The Populist Logic on the Environment

The Populist Logic on the Environment provides a framework that draws from populism's essence to explain populist politicians' approaches to the environment.

Over the past few decades, populism has spread across the world – particularly in Europe, but also notably in the US, South America, and Asia. Its essential features – especially its ideological 'thinness' – mean that we can observe considerable variations across populists in their environmental stances. This holds across the political spectrum from the left to the right, despite the traditional tendency of right-wing parties to be skeptical of pro-environmental positions and of left-wing parties to subscribe to them. Regardless of variations, however, 'true populists' can be expected to consistently anchor environmental stances in people-centrism and anti-elitism – in ways linked to additional party-specific factors. This book systematizes analytically what the literature observes, corrects some of its empirical limitations, and allows for reflection on the commitment by any one populist party to the environment. The authors undertake a cross-regional analysis of four case studies to illustrate their argument: Marine Le Pen's National Rally in France, the US Republican Party led by Donald Trump, Spain's Podemos led by Pablo Iglesias, and Hugo Chávez and Nicolás Maduro's socialist regime in Venezuela.

This book will appeal to scholars and students of political science, public policy, environmental studies, sociology, and geography, as well as a general audience interested in populism and the environment.

Francesco Duina is Charles A. Dana Professor in the Department of Sociology, and Social Sciences Division Chair, at Bates College, USA.

Hermione Xiaoqing Zhou is a Thomas J. Watson Fellow for 2023–2024.

Transforming Environmental Politics and Policy

Series Blurb

The theory and practice of environmental politics and policy are rapidly emerging as key areas of intense concern in the first, third and industrializing worlds. People of diverse nationalities, religions and cultures wrestle daily with environment and development issues central to human and non-human survival on the planet Earth. Air, Water, Earth, Fire. These central elements mix together in so many ways, spinning off new constellations of issues, ideas and actions, gathering under a multitude of banners: energy security, food sovereignty, climate change, genetic modification, environmental justice and sustainability, population growth, water quality and access, air pollution, maldistribution and over-consumption of scarce resources, the rights of the non-human, the welfare of future citizens-the list goes on.

What is much needed in green debates is for theoretical discussions to be rooted in policy outcomes and service delivery. So, while still engaging in the theoretical realm, this series also seeks to provide a 'real world' policy-making dimension. Politics and policy making is interpreted widely here to include the territories, discourses, instruments and domains of political parties, non-governmental organizations, protest movements, corporations, international regimes, and transnational networks.

From the local to the global-and back again-this series explores environmental politics and policy within countries and cultures, researching the ways in which green issues cross North-South and East-West divides. The 'Transforming Environmental Politics and Policy' series exposes the exciting ways in which environmental politics and policy can transform political relationships, in all their forms.

The Politics of Climate Change Knowledge
Labelling Climate Change-induced Uprooted People
Nowrin Tabassum

The Populist Logic on the Environment
Francesco Duina and Hermione Xiaoqing Zhou

For more information about this series, please visit: www.routledge.com/Transforming-Environmental-Politics-and-Policy/book-series/TEPP

The Populist Logic on the Environment

Francesco Duina and
Hermione Xiaoqing Zhou

Routledge
Taylor & Francis Group

LONDON AND NEW YORK

First published 2024
by Routledge
4 Park Square, Milton Park, Abingdon, Oxon OX14 4RN

and by Routledge
605 Third Avenue, New York, NY 10158

Routledge is an imprint of the Taylor & Francis Group, an informa business

British Library Cataloguing-in-Publication Data
A catalogue record for this book is available from the British Library

ISBN: 978-1-032-71664-0 (hbk)
ISBN: 978-1-032-72976-3 (pbk)
ISBN: 978-1-003-42313-3 (ebk)

DOI: 10.4324/9781003423133

Typeset in Times New Roman
by Apex CoVantage, LLC

Contents

Introduction

The Rise of Populism and the Environmental Question

How does populism relate to the environment? The existing research, even as it has expanded beyond its focus on Europe and right-wing populist parties that are negatively oriented towards the environment, tends to answer this by identifying empirical patterns emerging from the positions of selected populist parties. When it comes to the stances that those parties adopt, the results show interesting variations but these are not leveraged to propose an overall framework for how *populism itself* relates to environmental positions.

This book proposes by contrast a more general framework that draws from the essence of populism to articulate what we should expect in terms of the relationship between populism and the environment. While the literature tends to be inductive, we propose a more deductive approach – one that can in fact account for, in an analytically more systematic fashion, the observed variations in stances in the existing research and even correct some of its biases in terms of findings.

The core of our argument is the following. We start by noting the widely accepted view of populism as being ideologically 'thin' and primarily reliant for discursive purposes on the view that a 'pure people' (constructed by populists in specific and bounded ways using different imageries, such as 'those from the country's heartland,' the 'honest' and 'hard-working citizens,' or the 'true' members of a nation) suffers from the harmful actions of a 'corrupt elite' (also constructed to include a potential array of actors, such as the media, the political establishment, or international bureaucrats) (Mudde 2004, p. 543). As such, populism can subscribe to multiple positions regarding any particular substantive issue (Mudde and Kaltwasser 2013, 2017): that issue will be second-order and subservient to the overarching populist perspective. When it comes to the environment, or for that matter any other issue, this means that we can derive two expectations about the stances populists will take.

First, there is no *a priori* populist position on the environment. We should expect populist parties on the right end of the political spectrum to adopt negative but also positive stances, and the same can be said of their left-leaning counterparts. This is so regardless of the traditional tendency of right-wing parties to be skeptical of pro-environmental positions and of left-wing ones to be positively

DOI: 10.4324/9781003423133-1

inclined. Our first expectation, then, highlights the logical possibility of considerable variation in stances, even as we move across the traditional right versus left divide.

Second, notwithstanding such variations, we should also expect populist parties to share a key similarity, *in so far as they truly act as populist*. This is their anchoring of their environmental stances in the two core elements of populism: people-centrism and anti-elitism. Rather than determining specific positions, in other words, the populist logic demands that any one position be appropriated and justified in terms of these two core elements of populism. This is indeed what it means to be a populist: stances on any one issue are used to reaffirm to their audiences their commitment to 'the pure people' and disdain for 'the corrupt elite.' Our second expectation, then, concerns the embedding of environmental positions in the core message about the world that any given populist party wishes to project.

Importantly, such anchoring will acquire particular substantive content consonant with specific additional factors pertinent to that party: any ideological tendencies it subscribes to, its supporters' base, and the political and economic contexts in which it operates. This is what ultimately shapes the specific stances that any given populist party takes toward the environment. Indeed, these factors will also influence the selection of specific environmental issues – renewable energy, for instance, or the conservation of natural resources – that the party turns its attention to. The environment is, after all, not a monolithic subject matter. Populists will focus on those environmental issues that are in line with their overall profile. We note that existing research certainly already recognizes those factors as important, but does not link them analytically in a systematic fashion to the populist dimension of those parties.

To empirically support our argument, we examine the environmental stances of four populist parties: the French National Rally under Marine Le Pen (right-wing, pro-environment), the US Republican Party led by Donald Trump (right-wing, anti-environment), Spain's Podemos led by Pablo Iglesias (left-wing, pro-environment), and Hugo Chávez and Nicolás Maduro's populist Socialist regime in Venezuela (left-wing, anti-environment).

A number of implications follow from our proposed framework and analysis, including those related to the veracity of any given stance, the possibility of inconsistencies over time, and the policy impacts of such stances.

The book is organized as follows. Chapter 1 reviews the key findings and limitations of the existing research on populism and the environment. Chapter 2 presents our framework. Chapter 3 specifies the methods for the case study selection and analysis of the empirical materials. Chapters 4 through 7 focus on the case studies. Chapter 8 reflects on the implications of our framework and empirical analysis.

1 The Limits of the Existing Research on Populism and the Environment

Over the past few decades, populism has spread across the world (Inglehart and Norris 2016; Lewis, Barr, et al. 2019). Europe, in particular, has become a breeding ground for populist parties. In the 2018 round of European national elections, one in four votes was cast for populist parties compared to only 7% in 1998 (Lewis, Clarke, et al. 2019). More recent elections – for instance in Germany and Slovakia in 2023, France, Italy, Hungary, and Sweden in 2022, and Finland in 2019 – showed the continuing strength of those parties. In 2022, a record 32% of voters in 31 European countries cast ballots for populist parties – "a marked increase from 20% in the early 2000s and 12% in the early 1990s" (Henley 2023).

Populism has proliferated in other regions too. Examples include Donald Trump in the US, Jair Bolsonaro in Brazil, and Narendra Modi in India (Dieckhoff et al. 2022; Muno and Pfeiffer 2021; Stockemer 2019). In the summer of 2023, Tayyip Erdoğan won reelection as Turkey's president, while populist firebrand Javier Milei stunned observers by winning later in the year Argentina's presidential elections.

Scholars have responded by producing a sophisticated body of research on populism. Three major strands have developed (de la Torre 2019; Heinisch et al. 2021; Kaltwasser et al. 2017; Oswald 2022). One, by now well-developed, seeks to grasp populism's core features – above all, its people-centrism and anti-elitism (see, for instance, Mudde 2004, p. 544). A second identifies the possible causes of its growth. These range from 'supply' side ones (for instance, those emphasizing the ineffectiveness of traditional parties and the related growth of populist alternatives, or economic stagnation) to 'demand' side ones (for instance, the desire among voters to see new types of political leaders offering compelling solutions to existing problems) (Brubaker 2017; Inglehart and Norris 2016; Norris 2004). A third explores the position of populist parties on particular issues – such as immigration or minority rights (see, for instance, Akkerman 2012) – and, in some cases, the policy impacts of those positions (Mudde 2013).

It is in that third strand of literature that works on the stances of populist parties on the environment have started to emerge. A reading of these

DOI: 10.4324/9781003423133-2

works indicates that the primary mode of analysis has been 'bottom-up:' evidence from specific parties, typically in one geographical region, points to certain stances. We consider here the main findings, noting that they point to a fair amount of variation in stances, especially as research has expanded to consider cases beyond Europe. At the same time, by virtue of being largely inductive, those works highlight the observable empirical patterns but do not advance a general framework for how we should expect populism itself, *given its essential features*, to relate to the environment.

The most developed line of research in this third strand considers rightwing populist parties in Europe and identifies their negative orientations. This Europe-focused research can be organized into two subsets. The first focuses on party policy positions. The consensus is that European right-leaning populist parties oppose climate policies and treaties. Their nationalist appeals drive them to favor programs that prioritize economic growth and energy independence even if it means relying on nonrenewable sources (Forchtner 2019; Huber et al. 2021; Lockwood 2018; Schaller and Carius 2019; Selk and Kemmerzell 2022; Tosun and Debus 2021; Vihma et al. 2021). The results of those programs, scholars add, are negative for the environment (Böhmelt 2021; Jahn 2021; Riedel 2021; Otteni and Weisskircher 2022).

The second subset of Europe-focused works shifts the spotlight onto populist parties' supporters. The broadest analysis concerns data from 23 countries from the 2016 European Social Survey. Kulin et al. (2021) found that supporters of right-wing populism were more likely to hold nativist ideologies that correlated with higher levels of opposition to climate policies. In a similar vein, Yan et al. (2021) identified, based on survey responses and web browsing histories from six European countries, a link between support for right-wing populism and climate skepticism. Country-specific analyses have reached similar conclusions. A 2007–2016 longitudinal study in the UK, for instance, indicated that a "right-wing populist post-truth logic" has steered voters away from renewable energy alternatives (Batel and Devine-Wright 2018, p. 42).

The negative orientation of right-wing populist parties towards the environment seems confirmed by the smaller number of studies considering cases outside of Europe. These point to the prevalence of extractivist stances over conservational, renewable, or other pro-environmental issues (McCarthy 2019). Analyses of Mongolia (Myadar and Jackson 2019), the Philippines (Saguin 2019), the US with Donald Trump (Kojola 2019), and Brazil under President Jair Bolsonaro's philosophy of 'total extractivism' (Marquardt et al. 2022; Menezes and Barbosa Jr. 2021) offer examples.

Studies of left-wing populist parties, themselves fairly limited in numbers, also point to negative stances. The spotlight is usually on Latin America. The most revealing cases include Rafael Correa's 'petro-populism' in Ecuador (Lyall and Valdivia 2019), Mexican President Andrés Manuel López Obrador's prioritization of natural resource extraction at the expense of Indigenous communities (Solorio et al. 2021), and the extractive policies of Evo Morales's government in Bolivia (Andreucci 2018).

It may seem correct to conclude, based on the above research strands, that populist parties are not pro-environment. There are, however, a small but increasing number of studies of far-right populist parties that show support for certain pro-environmental policies in Europe under the guise of 'green patriotism' or other similar concepts (e.g. Caiani and Lubarda 2023; Ćetković and Hagemann 2020; François and Adrien 2021). These are complemented by one study of Ecuador's leftist populist government and its support of green policies in exchange for development support (Kramarz and Kingsbury 2022), and a brief discussion by Buzogány and Mohamad-Klotzbach (2022) suggesting that some left-leaning populists may in fact favor pro-environmental policies.

What should we take away, then, from the existing literature? The scholarship has produced valuable data suggesting multiple variations in stances – with negative ones seemingly more common. But it has one obvious shortcoming. The typical study focuses on selected right- or left-leaning parties in a given geographical region. Its objective is to determine inductively the position of those parties, and not the articulation of an overall understanding of how populism, given its essential features, relates to the environment. Given this, any conclusion that may be drawn from a survey of the various research findings seems analytically insufficient: we observe some trends but remain unclear about the relationship between *populism itself* and the environment.

In fact, it is worth noting that those articles that seek to account in causal terms for the observed positions often consider factors other than populism. Attention has gone primarily to right-wing anti-environment cases. One strand of argument sees 'structural' factors based on the economic needs of supporters as important (Lockwood 2018). A second points to 'ideological' factors such as "socially conservative, and nationalist values and their aversion to globalism, liberalism, and the loss of national sovereignty" (Buzogány and Mohamad-Klotzbach 2021, p. 157; see also Kojola 2019; Lockwood 2018; Saguin 2019). A third suggests that populist parties make expedient use of political opportunities (e.g. Oswald et al. 2021; Caiani and Lubarda 2023). These are, of course, valuable analyses pointing to influential factors, but they do not amount to *a priori* considerations of how populism itself, given its essential elements before any additional factors are brought into the picture, orients itself toward the environment.

The next chapter accordingly departs from the existing literature by specifying a more deductive approach – one that draws from populism's essence to articulate what we should expect when it comes to the environmental stances that populists adopt. Once that is understood, additional factors such as ideological leanings or supporters' bases can be introduced to determine how they become relevant in the context of that broader relationship.

2 A Framework for the Populist Logic on the Environment

We propose here that reflections on the nature of populism should help generate a set of expectations about its relationship to the environment. This deductive approach should in turn lead to a more complete and analytically informed understanding of what stances populist parties take and of how they take those stances – with important implications, discussed in Chapter 8, for the veracity of those stances, their consistency over time, and their practical impacts.

We accordingly start by identifying, based on the existing social scientific literature, the key features of populism. In the following section, we derive from those characteristics what we should, in principle, expect from populist parties when it comes to the environment.

The Key Characteristics of Populism

Numerous scholars have offered definitions of populism, especially if we turn to assessments made during manifestations of populism from decades prior to the current wave – such as those from late nineteenth century to the mid-twentieth century (Babson 2023). Most current social scientific perspectives, however, converge on a set of key characteristics even if some conceptual differences can certainly be noted (Mudde 2017, p. 27; see also Gallie 2019; Pellegrini 2023). These key characteristics can be organized into three categories: (1) those that highlight its ideological 'thinness' and discursive qualities, (2) those that identify its basic substantive worldview, and (3) those that specify how populism relates to the political establishment and direct democracy. What is stated about populism in any one category reinforces what is said in the other two. Taken together, they afford us with a useful set of insights that can generate expectations about populism and the environment.

Thin-Centered Ideology and Discursive Qualities

In his classic article, Mudde (2004, p. 544) defined populism as a "thin-centered ideology." Populism, he noted, exhibits "a restricted core attached to a narrower range of political concepts." As such, "it can be easily combined

DOI: 10.4324/9781003423133-3

with very different (thin and full) other ideologies, including communism, ecologism, nationalism or socialism." Taggart (2004, p. 274) expressed a very similar view when writing that populism "lacks core values." Any such core values, he added, are reflective of the people that the populist leader or party is supposed to represent and are not essential elements of populism itself. What those core values might be will, of course, in turn vary from case to case.

Put differently, populism needs a 'host' ideology. Its basic tenets can serve as foundations on which a number of other more developed ideological positions can rest. Given this, populist parties vary in terms of their views on political, economic, and social issues (Hawkins 2009), as well as in terms of political agendas, breaching traditional divisions such as those between right- and left-wing parties (e.g. Moffitt and Tormey 2014) and those between inclusive and exclusive positions toward particular minorities or groups in society (e.g. Duina and Carson 2019). Populism's malleability, Mudde and Kaltwasser (2013, 2017) have further noted, has facilitated its continued relevance across countries over the years: as conditions change, it can adapt by taking on new positions "cut[ting] across substantively quite different forms of politics" (Mudde and Kaltwasser 2013, p. 151).

It follows that populism may also be seen more as a 'discursive frame' than a programmatic phenomenon: it is primarily a 'political style,' 'repertoire of performance,' or 'political discursive logic' that amounts to a way of saying things rather than taking specific or elaborate substantive policy positions (Bonikowski 2016, p. 14; see also Curato 2017, p. 146; Staufer 2021, p. 225). If so, populism can also be viewed as a "strategic tool selected based on contexts" (Bonikowski 2016, p. 14) that becomes tailored to the "rhetoric, emotional appeals, embodied practices, and narratives" used by populist leaders across the traditional political spectrum (Kojola 2019, p. 373; see also Agnew and Shin 2017; Jansen 2011; Moffitt 2016). It serves as a convenient framing tool employed to varying degrees and intensities on different issues. Given that it is not equivalent to fixed political positions, any one politician may therefore be "'more or less' populist" at different times (Moffitt 2016, p. 21; see also Bonikowski 2016, p. 15), something that may not be as readily said about politicians of a more traditional cut, such as socialists or conservatives.

Basic Worldview

What, then, are the elements of this 'thin' ideology or discursive frame? Populists subscribe to certain basic perspectives on the world that are the conceptual building blocks on which everything else can be organized. The most important is the presentation of society as bifurcated into two groups: a morally pure and homogenous 'people' that is being harmed by a morally corrupt and equally homogenous 'elite' (Pellegrini 2023). As Mudde (2004, p. 543) put it, populism may be defined as a perspective "that considers society to be ultimately separated into two homogeneous and antagonistic groups, 'the pure people' versus 'the corrupt elite,' and which argues that politics should be an expression of the *volonté générale* (general will) of the people."

The "normative distinction between 'the elite' and 'the people'" is in this perspective crucial (Mudde 2004, p. 544). Populism entails a "Manichean outlook, in which there are only friends and foes. Opponents are not just those with different priorities and values, they are evil! Consequently, compromise is impossible, as it 'corrupts' the purity" of the people (ibid.; see also de la Torre 2018, p. 738; Oliver and Rahn 2016). The bifurcation, in other words, is predicated on an absolute moral distinction. Consequently, in this conflict there can be no middle ground or overlap between the two groups: populists are suspicious of any political, economic, or cultural claim the elites make as they vow to listen to and follow the common wisdom of the people (Mudde 2004; Oliver and Rahn 2016; Stanley 2008). The distinction is clear and "'the people' are understood as a bounded collectivity, and the basic contrast is between *inside* and *outside*" (Brubaker 2017, p. 363). Indeed, the primary role of populists is that of defenders of those boundaries (Agnew and Shin 2017; Balthazar 2017; Kenny 2017).

Of course, what qualifies as 'the people' and 'the elite' is far from given. These are not natural categorizations easily deployed in any given social context, nor is it obvious from the start where the boundaries between those categories begin or end. Populists go to great lengths to construct, and if useful to later modify, the identities of both groups in their binary rhetoric (Mudde 2004, p. 548–550). In fact, Laclau (2005a) goes as far as to suggest that populism is the process through which 'the people' are repeatedly named, defined, and articulated by populists in juxtaposition to 'the elite' (see also Laclau 2005b; Moffitt 2016, p. 23–24). Bonikowski (2016, p. 10) in turn has proposed that populist leaders purposefully choose not to specify the scope of 'the people' in order to maximize their base. Rather, they refer to 'the people' as everyone but 'the elite,' with whom they exist in fundamental antagonism. The same may be said about 'the elite' – the label is fairly void of specificity and populists engage in naming and renaming of who belongs to it in light of what seems most useful.

With that said, the populist depiction of 'the elite' and 'the people' has certain clearly defined qualities. The designation of 'elite' is assigned to individuals who hold certain levels of power, authority, or privilege in society (ibid.). These may include the media, politicians, business leaders, or intellectuals. They exert a disproportionate amount of control over the operations and organization of things. Their claims to privileged positions may be legitimate, but this does not prevent populists from vilifying them and describing them as the enemy of the people. Indeed, the fundamental 'problem' of the people is the "elites' abandonment of the common good in favor of their own self-interest" (ibid., p. 11). The elites are selfish, corrupt, and out of touch with the real people, and blamed for their plight.

The elites may be found within the nation but also outside of it – as global capitalists or international bureaucrats, for instance (Brubaker 2017, p. 363). Moreover, the elites may also be seen as closely connected to 'other groups' who do not belong to the upper strata of society but are nonetheless beneficiaries of the elites' actions – and as such are at times conceptually conflated with them. These might be people of color, immigrants, or even criminals (ibid.; de la Torre 2018, p. 744). Together with the elite, they constitute a 'dangerous other' or 'enemy' that collectively is "depriving (or attempting to deprive) the sovereign people of their rights, values, prosperity, identity, and voice" (Albertazzi and McDonnell 2008, p. 3).

If the elites are evil, 'the pure people' are glorified as decent, diligent, and honest. They rely on common sense and see things as they really are. As a whole, they form "a homogeneous and virtuous community" (Mudde and Kaltwasser 2013, p. 151). At the same time, they are portrayed as the victims of elites' actions – who ignore, silence, and exploit them to advance their agendas. 'The people' can include hardworking citizens, everyday folks, the 'true' or 'genuine' members of a nation, and other similar groups of people. As we move from left-leaning to right-leaning populists, the makeup exhibits some of the most marked differences. For the latter populist types, for instance, the overlap between 'the people' and 'the nation' can be total. As Mudde (2004, p. 549) writes, for them "the step from 'the nation' to 'the people' is easily taken, and the distinction between the two is often far from clear." The nation, in turn, is understood to involve ethnic, historical, or cultural determinants. But a sense of 'the people' as 'nation' can also be found among left-leaning populists. In those cases, however, what is understood by the nation is something more open and expansive (hence immigrants might belong to it, or anyone belonging to the working class), less exclusionary, and ultimately related to some aspect of their working-class status or at least less privileged position in the economic system compared to wealthier members of society (Duina and Carson 2019; de la Torre 2018, p. 744).

To these descriptors of 'the people' we may add the concept of the 'heartland' (Taggart 2004, p. 274). The people belong to it. The heartland, in turn, "represents an idealized conception of the community they [populists] serve. It is from this territory of the imagination that populists construct the 'people' as the object of their politics." This may be more common among right-leaning populists. The heartland appeals as a primordial basis for individuals' shared identity constructed from an idealized past for which the people are nostalgic, and the populists aim to bring back a desirable past with "a good life before the corruptions and distortions of the present" (ibid.; see also Taggart 2000). Of course, here too the people belonging to the heartland undergo an endless process of being named and defined, as "heartlands are something that is felt rather than reasoned . . . different positions can implicitly conjure up heartlands that differ from each other" (Taggart 2004, p. 274).

This bifurcated view of the world allows populists to claim their mission: they are the true representatives of the people. While they may have more power than the people, they acquire and deploy it "on behalf of the people" (Bonikowski 2016, p. 11; see also Mudde 2004, p. 558). As such, "they speak for the 'silent majority' of 'ordinary, decent people' whose interests and opinions are (they claim) regularly overridden by arrogant elites, corrupt politicians, and strident minorities" (Canovan 1999, p. 5).

Anti-Establishment and Direct Democracy

Such views on 'the pure people' and 'the morally corrupt elite' directly inform how populists position themselves toward the political system. Despite their often aggressive language and promises of radical change, populists actually often do not seek a whole rewrite of the social order: they are "reformist rather than revolutionary" (Mudde 2004, p. 546). This is because they do "not want to change the people themselves, but rather their status within the political system" (ibid.). Put differently, populists claim that the political system has been captured by the elites and rendered ineffective or outright harmful. What is therefore needed is a cleansing of that system from the elites and the consequences of their actions. This means that populists make two sorts of claims about themselves and the system.

The first entails the rejection of the existing political leadership, legislators, and even judges and administrators. The 'establishment' must be challenged and curtailed. The 'swamp,' as President Donald Trump's slogan went, must be 'drained.' The moral rot brought about by the elites must be replaced by a healthier set of political actors who, to start at least, should be 'outsiders.' At the helm of that movement, of course, are the populist leaders themselves. They present "themselves as the exact opposites of the established parties . . . championing the common sense and decent values of 'the people'" (ibid., p. 548). Accordingly, existing legislative representatives, judges, and administrators should be opposed.

The second follows closely from the first. Populists claim to be representative of the people. As such, they favor a direct type of democracy over a representative one. The will of the majority must be the guiding principle and the reason to "reassert democratic political control" (Brubaker 2017, p. 364). Hence, referendums are seen as valuable, as are unfiltered channels of communication between the people and the leaders themselves that function as "direct, unmediated, institutionalized support from large numbers of mostly unorganized followers" (Weyland 2001, p. 14). The objective is "the replacement of existing intermediate political institutions with more direct forms of participation" (Bonikowski 2016, p. 11). Minorities may therefore in the process lose some voice or relevance, but that is acceptable and indeed to be expected when "popular sovereignty" is seen as "the only legitimate source of political power" (Mudde and Kaltwasser 2013, p. 151).

The combination of anti-establishment sentiments and calls for direct democracy has various implications. Among the most important is that populism tends to be "reductive," and opposed to "nuanced political arguments in favor of moral outrage" (Bonikowski 2016, p. 22). It encourages "politics based on fear and resentment rather than informed policy debate" (ibid.). It also means a propensity for populist leaders to exhibit charismatic qualities. These sorts of leaders distinguish themselves by emphasizing that they are outsiders of the establishment – and as such especially qualified to advance the true interests of the people.

The Populist Logic on the Environment

The previous section affords us sufficient analytical insights into populism to generate two key expectations about how populists might orient themselves towards the environment. We begin, however, by first specifying what we mean by environmental 'stances.' Environmental stances are substantive positions toward the environment. Consistent with the coding approach used in databases such as MARPOR (a project funded by the German Science Foundation and considered one of the best databases in comparative politics) where scholars define what is meant by the environmental positions of political parties,[1] we define the term environmental 'stances' as positions related to the use, exploitation, or preservation of natural resources (e.g. fossil fuels, underground minerals), climate change, air and water pollution, energy generation, land use, and biodiversity. Thus, examples of pro-environmental stances include a commitment to renewable energy, international climate treaties, and resource conservation. Examples of anti-environmental stances by contrast include support for resource extraction, deregulation of practices that can harm the environment, and continued fossil fuels reliance. Stances can accordingly be found in statements as well as policies, and they should be distinguished from 'impacts' – a point to which we will return in Chapter 8.

We can now turn to our preceding discussions of populism to generate two expectations about the environmental stances of populist parties. *First*, there is no set of *a priori* environmental stances inherent to the populist mindset. As we saw, populism is ideologically 'thin.' It offers an elementary narrative that divides the social world into two parts. As is the case for many other substantive policy issues, the environment is therefore of second-order importance. Accordingly, if we consider the traditional political spectrum from left to right (the most typical axis of differences when it comes to the environment), we should expect populist parties on the right-end of the political spectrum to take on negative but also positive stances, and the same can be said of their left-leaning counterparts. This is so even if traditionally right-leaning parties may be said to be less inclined toward the environment, while their left-leaning counterparts have been more positively oriented. After all, populists are right-leaning, *as populists*, only in their understanding of 'the people' as consisting of a 'nation' defined by ethnic, cultural, or historical factors, and of the 'elites' as those in positions of privilege and power who have been intent on undermining the well-being of 'the people' so defined. And they are left-leaning, *as populists*, in their more inclusive understanding of 'the people' that tends to see them as placed lower in the economic system – as 'working-class' or 'hardworking' citizens, for instance – and of 'the elite' as those who have taken advantage of the people primarily in economic terms. When it comes to any given policy issue, populists are inherently flexible. Any one position may be worked within the basic populist worldview. This explains with analytical clarity why the existing research on specific populist parties points to a variety of environmental positions: the variation is logically consistent with the nature of populism.

To this, we can add a *second* expectation. Notwithstanding the possible variations in stances, we should expect populist parties to share a key similarity, *in so far as they truly act as populists*. They will anchor their environmental stances in the two core elements of populism: people-centrism and anti-elitism. Rather than determining specific positions, the populist logic demands instead that any one position be appropriated and justified in terms of the core elements of populism's worldview. *This is indeed what it means to be a populist: their stances on any given environmental matter will be used to reaffirm to their audiences their commitment to 'the pure people' and disdain of 'the corrupt elite.'* Existing research at times depicts cases of such rhetorical work, but not explicitly as an essential derivative of the logic of populism itself that should be observed across all cases of genuine populist behavior.

Importantly, such anchoring will acquire particular substantive content consonant with the specific additional factors pertinent to that party. This will help determine the specific environmental positions that the party will take – for instance pro-renewable energy or against the protection of natural landscapes. The factors include the ideological tendencies the party subscribes to. Recall that populism, as an ideologically 'thin' phenomenon, usually places itself in a more developed ideological 'home' – most obviously one situated along the right versus left spectrum but, of course, also other dimensions such as for or against globalization. The values championed by those ideologies inform how populists carry out their primary objective of projecting their bifurcated view of the world, including when this involves putting forth environmental stances. For instance, a right-leaning party might declare its support for protected national parks as part of a discourse of national greatness and in reaction to the harmful actions of previous government elites who did little to protect the integrity of the country, while a left-leaning one might promote the exploitation of fossil fuels by invoking ideas of self-sufficiency and the need to protect economically hardworking and honest citizens from the harms caused by transnational capitalism and markets.

A second factor is the party's base of supporters. Populists must resonate with their followers. Their base will logically orient them toward certain specific environmental positions. Put differently, in their anchoring work populists must put forth particular environmental ideas that will be accepted, and in fact reflect, what their followers value. Thus, if voters are worried about the environment (or certain aspects of the many challenges it is facing), we can expect populist parties to take favorable positions toward pro-environmental stances. The opposite holds true in turn – with populists taking anti-environmental stances if this seems consistent with supporters' preferences, as might be the case, for instance, when significant numbers of those supporters work in extractive industries.

The political and economic contexts in which the party operates constitute the additional key factors. Politically, whether parties are operating in democracies or single-party systems, as part of government or in opposition, at times of stability or instability, and other similar considerations will inform their anchoring work. Economically, the same may be said when it comes to whether they operate in market or command economies, in times of growth or recession, with low or high levels of unemployment, in a resource-rich country or not, and other such matters. We note that these are, in fact, many of the factors that existing research on populism already lists when seeking to explain the environmental stances of the populist parties that are being analyzed – but that those works do not specify analytically in a systematic fashion how these factors connect to the populism of those parties as a general conceptual construct.

Importantly, the above means that any one populist party will likely be selective in the choice of specific environmental issues – renewable energy, for instance, or the conservation of natural resources – that it will consider. As our earlier definition of 'stances' indicated, the environment is not a monolithic subject matter. Populists will focus on those environmental issues that are substantively consonant with their overall profile and take stances in accordance with that profile.

If we are correct, we should see these expected dynamics around variation and anchoring work in actual cases of populism. As we do this, we can also expect populists to be dismissive of the 'establishment' and representative democratic institutions. This will be part of their championing of 'the pure people' and condemnation of 'the morally corrupt elites.' The next section specifies the methodology for our empirical investigation.

Before proceeding, we note that a number of implications follow from our proposed framework and analysis, including those related to the veracity of any given stance, the possibility of inconsistencies over time, and the policy impacts of such stances. We will discuss those in the final chapter of this book. What is important to underline here is that our proposed framework is not concerned with the extent to which populists are truly committed to their environmental stances. We recognize that their rhetoric may be opportunistic, for instance. Our main point is a different one: if populists include the environment in their rhetoric, the logic of their populism tells us that they can take either pro- or anti-environmental stances and, in so doing, that they will ground their positions in their people-centrism and anti-elitism. Our goal in the empirical chapters ahead is to shed light on the relationship between the essence of populism and the environmental stances of populists.

Notes

1 See https://manifesto-project.wzb.eu/coding_schemes/mp_v4. *The variable for the environment is variable 501 (Environmental Protection: Positive) and is defined as:*

• *General policies in favor of protecting the environment, fighting climate change, and other 'green' policies. For instance:*

   • *General preservation of natural resources;*
   • *Preservation of countryside, forests, etc.;*
   • *Protection of national parks;*
   • *Animal rights.*

• *May include a great variance of policies that have the unified goal of environmental protection.*

3 Methodology

We aim to present empirical data in support of the two expectations derived from our proposed framework: (1) variation in environmental stances across both left-leaning and right-leaning populist parties and (2) a consistent anchoring of those varying stances in people-centrism and anti-elitism, with connections to factors specific to each party that help define its stances. Given this, we chose to rely on an in-depth analysis of selected case studies. We selected case studies according to several principles that can help maximize the relevance of the findings. We note that small N studies are typical in comparative case analyses across geographies when the objective is not to reach statistical generalizability but, rather, an in-depth understanding of the dynamics involved in the phenomenon of interest (Köllner et al. 2018, p. 4).

We selected four case studies: one for each expected combination of left-/ right-wing and pro-/anti-environment. More case studies illustrative of each variation would of course be useful, but limitations of space require a more parsimonious approach. These are intrinsically important cases (Odell 2003): populist parties that are clearly either right- or left-leaning and have enjoyed considerable electoral successes in their countries. We wish to consider, in other words, prominent cases for the expected variations.

The cases should at the same time be different from each other when it comes to the specific ideological positions they embrace, their supporters' bases, and the economic and political contexts in which they operate. This will grant more validity to the investigation of how populist parties consistently anchor their environmental stances in the core populist elements of people-centrism and anti-elitism. This means that we should consider parties in Europe but also beyond. Comparative politics scholars emphasize that "contextualized comparison of similarly defined units selected from different world regions" helps capture the presence and characteristics of proposed dynamics while recognizing the particularities of each individual case (Köllner et al. 2018, p. 18).

Additionally, we should also select cases that offer clear and ample empirical materials (assertions in the media, speeches, manifestos, etc.) that are revealing of the logic behind their positions. This will improve the accuracy of the resulting takeaways.

DOI: 10.4324/9781003423133-4

In light of the above considerations, Table 3.1 identifies the four case studies for analysis. They are prominent populist parties that have operated in Europe, North America, and Latin America in remarkably different political and economic settings. They subscribe to rather different ideologies (right- vs. left-leaning, and also within those categories), and rely on different bases of supporters. And, of course, they represent the four possible combinations of political leaning (right vs. left) and environmental stances (positive vs. negative) we are most interested in illustrating and understanding. Finally, they offer material that permits an exploration of their anchoring logic.

We note again that other cases could have been selected. We selected these four because they are especially fitting. In the case of Latin America, for instance, the parties of Rafael Correa in Ecuador or Evo Morales in

Table 3.1 Case Study Selection

	Pro-environment	Anti-environment
Right-wing	National Rally with Marine Le Pen, France Ideology: Neofascist, xenophobic, localist Supporters' base: Disaffected citizens worried about the preservation of 'traditional' French society and the influences of international forces Economic and political contexts: Growing anti-EU sentiments, deep farming and food traditions with strong popular support, rejection of traditional political parties	Republican Party with Donald Trump, USA Ideology: Neoliberal, nationalist, protectionist Supporters' base: Americans from the 'heartland' feeling betrayed by the nation's elites, harmed by unfair international competition, and eager to bring back America's 'greatness' Economic and political contexts: Abundant natural resources, global hegemon, anti-globalization sentiments
Left-wing	Podemos with Pablo Iglesias, Spain Ideology: Socialist, anti-market, youth- and working-class oriented Supporters' base: Young and other Spaniards worried about economic insecurities, political corruption, and true democratic representation Economic and political contexts: Market economy, high youth unemployment, 80-year-long bipartisan deadlock	Hugo Chávez's and Nicolás Maduro's United Socialist Party of Venezuela Ideology: Socialist, anti-imperialist, for self-sufficiency Supporters' base: Working-class Venezuelans against the international neoliberal order and looking for an end to poverty and for widespread redistribution of wealth Economic and political contexts: Fossil fuel economy, developing economy, struggling working class, single-party regime

Bolivia would have satisfied the selection criteria. But Chávez is considered by many scholars and other observers to be the quintessential Latin America populist leader of the last two or three decades (e.g. Hawkins 2009; Sagarzazu and Thies 2019; Zúquete 2008). "However populism was defined," notes a scholar of Latin American politics, "Chávez fit, as he seemingly embodied whatever core and ancillary properties were attached to the concept" (Roberts 2012, p. 136). The Venezuelan case was accordingly selected.

As already noted in Chapter 2, we define pro-environment stances as statements and policies that support a range of environmental protection and conservation measures. Anti-environment stances are statements and policies that by contrast reject environmental protection and conservation measures. Importantly, as noted in Chapter 2, the focus is on conceptual positions and therefore not on policy impacts, though along the way some attention will be given to such impacts in so far as they are derivatives of those positions. We will return to this distinction in Chapter 8 and the question of what actual impacts populist parties might be expected to have, especially when they occupy positions of power.

To identify the environmental stances of the four selected parties, we analyzed textual materials from those parties (policy platforms, official statements, press releases, websites, etc.) as well as audio and visual materials (interviews, rallies, campaign videos, etc.). To find and access those materials, we relied on wide-open Internet searches, parties' official websites and channels of communication, government archives and other sources, searches of various media channels (YouTube, Twitter, etc.), websites of international organizations such as the United Nations, news sources (as available on the Internet but also Nexis-Uni and other databases), and websites of governmental and nongovernmental organizations. When helpful, secondary sources with valuable assertions or passages from populist leaders or parties were consulted.

As suggested already, the materials ultimately selected for inclusion in this book were intended to be neither comprehensive nor random, but to be instead the most relevant and revealing about the environmental stances of those parties. With this said, we stress here that we collected as much potentially relevant data as possible for initial analysis, and continued to consider data points until we reached 'saturation' in the themes we encountered and a synthesis was therefore possible.

Time periods considered cover when those parties articulated their environmental stances. With all relevant materials, our goal was to identify passages and images that contained either pro- or anti-environmental stances, and passages where populist actors anchored those stances in their people-centric or anti-elitist perspectives. We collected those passages to arrive at a picture of their overall tendencies, and accordingly present the resulting picture in the chapters ahead.

Materials in French or Spanish were translated by one of the authors who can read those languages. Google Translate and DeepL were consulted as needed if further translation input was useful.

We begin with right-wing populists and proceed to their left-wing counterparts. We observe the remarkable variations in their stances, and we examine their anchoring in people-centrism and anti-elitism in ways reflective of their ideologies, supporters' bases, and broader economic and political contexts.

4   Right-Wing and Pro-Environment in France

National Rally's Nationalistic Green Localism

This chapter considers France's leading right-wing populist party National Rally (*Rassemblement National*, [RN]) – formerly known as National Front (*Front National*) – under the leadership of Marine Le Pen until 2022. RN's prominent presence in French politics and Le Pen's nearly successful 2017 and 2022 presidential campaigns make it a leading example of Europe's recent populist surge. For our purposes, it is the representative case of a right-wing populist party that has taken pro-environmental positions – offering a valuable illustration of the variety of positions populists can take toward the environment.

This chapter is divided into sections. We begin by identifying those positions. We then examine RN's anchoring of those stances in its populism: RN embedded those stances in its people-centrism and anti-elitism. The stances became material for RN to project its bifurcated worldview – in ways that were consonant with its ideological 'home,' its supporters' base, and the economic and political contexts in which RN has operated.

RN's Pro-Environmentalism

RN's conservative profile might lead observers to presume that it should exhibit a general opposition to pro-environmental policies. As it turns out, starting in 2014, when most far-right populist parties in Europe were preoccupied with campaigning against Green parties for electoral support, RN began to take an unexpected turn toward pro-environmental positions. RN's stances emphasized an attachment to land, ecology, and local farming. They featured a rejection of global capitalism and large-scale commercial interests as harmful to nature, and portrayed instead the environmental benefits stemming from smaller scale enterprises and initiatives. Those who live and work on the land, RN posited, know best what is needed for its preservation. The relationship was thus presented as symbiotic. Scale mattered in this regard: French farmers should be supported, while products and ideas coming from 'outside' France or large corporations should be distrusted and closely

DOI: 10.4324/9781003423133-5

scrutinized. Accordingly, RN also expressed support for environmental measures that provided tangible improvements to local living spaces and activities – green zones in urban centers, for instance, or energy-saving programs such as the city-wide installation of LED light bulbs. In parallel, RN promoted certain forms of renewable energy and other initiatives on a national scale that would safeguard France's 'sovereignty' while supporting domestic employment and incomes.

We can see these stances being first articulated in RN's 2014 *New Ecology* (*Nouvelle Écologie*) movement. It presented a combination of priorities as "a 'patriotic' and 'realistic' response to climate change" and a localized alternative to ineffective international climate governance (de Nadal 2021). As Mireille d'Ornano, a member of the European Parliament and of its Committee on the Environment, Public Health and Food Safety, stated, "the New Ecology movement is based on national interest and patriotism." She accordingly dismissed the UN Framework Convention on Climate Change, the international climate talks process, as a "communist project," stressing that "we don't want a global agreement or global rule for the environment" (Neslen 2014). Describing itself as made up of "the very people who are so attached to the flora, fauna and landscapes of our beautiful country," RN stated its opposition to the extraction of shale gas (Machin and Wagener 2019). Instead, it called for the exploitation of methane from agricultural waste and related 'conservation agriculture' measures. Broader initiatives that could promote France's energy autonomy were also envisioned. In that vein, two members of parliament, Gilbert Collard and Marion Maréchal-Le Pen, introduced an amendment to the French energy transition bill championing the country's extensive nuclear power sector as worth saving and not abandoning (Martin 2014). Describing that sector as "as a central pillar in the objectives of reducing greenhouse gas emissions," the amendment emphasized that it helped make France less dependent on foreign oil and gas. "The French nuclear assets," the amendment continued, "ensures energy independence for our nation while being a guarantee of security and respect for the environmental commitments to which France has subscribed" (Assemblée Nationale 2014).

The *New Ecology* movement eventually gave way to additional pro-environmental positions as articulated in Le Pen's *144 Presidential Commitments (144 Engagements Présidentiels)* of 2017, which were developed for her presidential campaign. Presented as numbers 131 to 137, they included a promise "to preserve the environment" by "break[ing] with the economic model founded on wild globalization trade, and social, health, and environmental dumping," adding that "true ecology consists of producing and consuming as locally as possible." They called for the massive development of solar power and biofuels "thanks to a smart protectionism" that would also see the development of a French hydrogen sector. Additionally, they sought to outlaw shale gas, make animal protection and the precautionary principle for genetically modified organisms priorities, and support a home insulation program (Le Pen 2017a).

Later, in 2021, in its *15 Questions on the Environment, Counter-Project Referendum* (*15 Questions Sur L'Environnement, Conter-Project de Référendum*), RN proposed new environmental directions countering those of Macron's 2021 plan (Rassemblement National 2021). This was in response to the government's proposed constitutional climate bill under consideration in the National Assembly (Damiani and Pollet 2021). The referendum posed 15 questions, to be answered by the French people and to be used to revise the Constitution and existing laws (Durand 2021; Rassemblement National 2021, p. 3). These were the 15 questions on the referendum. Le Pen, importantly, suggested that citizens should answer each positively (Rassemblement National 2021, p. 7) – thus stating RN's positions on these matters:

1   Would you like our constitutional texts to contain the principle of environmental security and the protection of our tangible and intangible heritage?
2   Would you like to see the general introduction of detailed labeling for food products?
3   Would you like France to continue investing in nuclear, carbon-free energy?
4   Do you want parent companies to be responsible for environmental damage caused by their subsidiaries?
5   Do you want the construction of infrastructure or collective facilities of national interest to be submitted to Parliament for approval?
6   Do you want acts taken within the framework of the European Union which do not respect the provisions of the environmental charter to be inapplicable in France?
7   Do you wish to suspend all wind turbine construction projects?
8   Do you wish to suspend the installation of all large-scale projects?
9   Would you like to severely restrict all new construction on agricultural land?
10   Do you want to develop green spaces in cities and green and blue networks by putting in place constraints for municipalities?
11   Would you like to see farmers paid for the upkeep of 'natural carbon storage areas?'
12   Do you want to ban imports of products (agricultural or manufactured) whose manufacture or production is prohibited in France?
13   Would you like VAT [Value Added Tax] to vary according to whether products can be repaired and recycled?
14   Would you like France to introduce a tax on imported products to compensate for the effects of their production and transport on the environment?
15   Would you like the importer or distributor to be held liable in the event of the sale on the French market of a product that is defective or does not comply with the regulations in force?

(Rassemblement National 2021, p. 19)

Consistent with prior initiatives, these questions pointed to a fairly specific set of positions toward the environment. They prioritized farmers and green spaces in towns and villages, shunned large-scale projects, mixed environmental protection with security, and targeted business and external actors for their impact on the environment.

Anchoring Work

How should we understand these noteworthy pro-environmental stances? Rather than seeing them as primary commitments to the environment, we should view them as intrinsically connected to RN's populist people-centrism and anti-elitism. RN used these stances to express its populism: they were substantive points, consonant with its overall profile, leveraged to forcefully project its essential view of the world. Overall, that view revolved around a depiction of France as having suffered greatly at the hands of morally corrupt domestic and international elites who had sought to advance an environmental agenda that had served their interests to the detriment of the honest, good people of France – including their wellbeing, livelihood, and connections to the land. RN's pro-environmentalism was therefore part of its efforts to rescue the French people from imminent disaster and grant them what they wanted and deserved.

Of course, as stressed in the preceding chapter, we need not assume here that the stances were necessarily genuine, or that they did not represent opportunistic moves. In fact, our framework suggests that, by virtue of its ideological 'thinness,' populism is not inherently committed to any one position. These are important questions in their own right to which we will return in Chapter 8. Let us analyze each anchoring element in turn. First, however, it will be helpful to provide some basic data points about RN's profile.

In terms of ideology, as we have discussed, by virtue of their ideological 'thinness' all populist parties 'house' themselves in more developed ideological platforms. *RN* was no exception. Its ideological home consisted of a staunchly nationalistic and nativist set of claims about the importance of defending the foundational values of the French Republic – Liberty, Equality, Fraternity – against the purported threats posed by "massive immigration" bringing foreign cultures to France (Kaya 2021; see also Sandford 2017; Surel 2019). Thus, RN subscribed to an anti-immigration platform, calling for a "revolution of proximity, local before global" (Le Pen 2017b) and vouching to protect the "one language, one culture" within the "one [French] national community" (Sandford 2017).

Along these lines, Le Pen described the central political conflict of the time as having "no longer put the right and left in opposition, but patriots and globalists" (ibid.). As she stated, her opponents who support globalization "made an ideology out of it. An economic globalism which rejects all limits, all regulation of globalization, and which consequently weakens the immune defenses of the nation state, dispossessing it of its constituent elements: borders, national currency, the authority of its laws and management of the economy, thus enabling another globalism to be born and to grow – Islamist fundamentalism" (ibid.). RN set itself directly against such values. It was conservative and, with that, patriotic, anti-globalization, pro-state, and categorically secular. As she put it in her *144 Presidential Commitments* published for the upcoming elections:

> This presidential election will bring two visions face to face. The 'globalist' choice on the one hand, represented by all my competitors, which seeks to destroy our great economic and social balances, which wants the abolition of all borders, both economic and physical, and which wants ever more immigration and less cohesion between the French. The patriotic choice on the other, which I embody in this election, which puts the defense of the nation and the people at the heart of all public decisions and which above all wants the protection of our national identity, our independence, the unity of the French, social justice and prosperity for all. (Le Pen 2017a, p. 2)

To this she added that "I also want to give the French people their money back, because for too many years, our social and fiscal policies have impoverished the middle and working classes, while enriching the multinationals and squandering public money" (ibid.). The state should be serving France's citizens, not other entities or causes (Surel 2019).

In terms of its base, RN's supporters were accordingly by and large disaffected segments of the population who were eager to 'preserve' French society and save it from the destructive influences of international factors. Its voters tended to be in rural areas or smaller cities, with those unemployed and with a lower level of education showing a particular interest in its policy proposals (Aisch et al. 2017; Wike 2017). RN also won a significant portion of the working class electorate as well as the young (Surel 2019), and received strong support among those holding unfavorable views of migrants, Muslims, and participation in the global economy (Wike 2017). Over time, as it has sought to broaden its appeal, RN has made inroads among selected disadvantaged groups such as gays and women (Duina and Carson 2019). Additionally, as RN gained prominence and seats in the National Assembly and local elections in the early 2020s, and as the need to tackle the environmental crisis became a major concern of French voters for both political and economic reasons, RN spoke with some success to those concerned with certain aspects of the environmental crisis (Guillou 2022).

RN's successes must, of course, be seen in the broader economic and political changes shaping France in the last few decades. There were growing anti-EU sentiments (Goodliffe 2014). The country had deep farming and food traditions that received strong popular support and benefited from powerful lobbyists at the national and international levels. Recent elections were in parallel seen as the rejection of traditional political parties, with the implosion of the traditional conservative and socialist parties. Voters abandoned those parties and looked for alternatives – the RN, of course, but also Macron's The Republic on the Move *(La République en Marche)* (which in 2022 changed its name to *Renaissance*). Economically, the country was struggling with growth, widening inequalities, and mass protests against government attempts to liberalize the economy and lower social benefits (Kaya 2021; Goodliffe 2014).

Anti-Elitism

We can start with RN's anchoring of its pro-environmental stances in its anti-elitism. Its pro-environmental stances were presented as necessary extensions of Le Pen's slogan 'the revolution of proximity, local before global.' The aim was to frame its own pro-environmental initiatives as responses to the environmentalism of corrupt elites who had developed and then imposed on France a series of ineffective and harmful environmental policies. In this effort, RN targeted three layers of elites.

The first layer was the global elite. RN envisioned local environmental initiatives as protecting France from intrusive and ineffective global environmentalists who, according to Hervé Juvin (2019), an RN representative in the European Parliament and a key RN voice, "do not know borders nor the sovereignty of States, any more than democracy!" Rather, their "ecological requirements are diverted for the benefit of multinationals and dominant players, quite simply by the complexity of the rules and standards" (ibid.). Hence, RN launched a fierce campaign against global environmental governance as ineffective and corrupt. Juvin painted the *Paris Agreement*, for instance, as a "failure," "a symbol of the impotence of the great globalist machines," whose "objectives will not be met" despite the "resounding communiques." After all, "most of the participants do not even take the desired direction!" (ibid.). That machine is closely connected to the "economic model of globalized free trade, which is structurally bad for the environment" and something that "push[es] the lowest environmental bidder," causing among other things transport-generated pollution (Front National 2015; Le Pen 2017c). Indeed, according to RN, "the reduction of greenhouse gasses would in fact be increased tenfold if we agreed to call into question an economic model of globalized free trade, which is structurally bad for the environment," and therefore also bad for the French people (Front National 2015).

Juvin (2019) further depicted global environmental initiatives as part of "the globalist swindle that hides behind the climate alert campaign." The 'swindle' must be countered with 'true' ecology, which "is a matter of locality, singularities, and collective choices" taken within the French borders. As Juvin explained, when the globalists asserted that "since climate change does not stop at borders, the solutions are global," that "can only come from global organizations" who do not understand genuine democracy, "the borders, or the sovereignty of states." Le Pen (2017b) herself asserted something similar in Lyon in 2017, at her Presidential Campaign Launch. As she put it:

> Who could possibly believe, as the adepts of globalization proclaim, that it would be logical, environmentally friendly, or even economically sustainable to produce on one continent, transform on another, and consume on a third? We want a sustainable economy for France. We can achieve the relocation of our production by a reasonable and calculated use of economic protectionism and by applying economic patriotism. These are normal economic tools although they are currently prohibited by the European Union.

The second layer of elites were, therefore, EU officials and other Europeanists. Consistent with its 'Frexit' campaign that called for France's exit from the EU, RN tied the EU's weak environmental actions to the "deficiencies of the Brussels technocracy" and the "ineffective and dangerous supranational mechanisms [of the EU], where decisions and actions are imposed from above on nations and therefore on peoples" (Odoul 2018; Collectif Nouvelle Ecologie 2016). Accordingly, the EU's failure to enforce strict diesel standards showed "the disproportionate weight of lobbies in the decisions of the European Commission . . . [who] lied and did not protect the Europeans" (Collectif Nouvelle Ecologie 2015). In another example, RN "consider[ed] the definition of endocrine disruptors presented by the European Commission unacceptable . . . the protection of living organisms and consumers cannot be achieved within the framework of the European Union" (Murer and Richermoz 2016). In yet another example, RN attacked the EU's belated action on banning bee-killing pesticides by "denounc[ing] the deadly deficiencies of the Brussels technocracy" and claiming that "this ban is a salvation for professionals but the damage to our ecosystems is immense and partly irreversible" (Odoul 2018). Thus, Juvin (2019) stressed, "the financial world [is] rubbing its hands at the idea of the hundreds of billions that the [European] Union is committed to spending on objectives that are as uncertain as they are distant – the commissions of the financial intermediaries will be very real, as will the incomes of the NGOs and agencies that will award them their certificate of good ecological conduct!"

Countering these supposedly failed international environmental actions, RN presented its own 'nationalistic green localism' (Juvin 2019; see also Milman 2021; Baléo 2020), for which "borders are the environment's greatest ally; it is through them that we will save the planet" (Mazoue 2019). "Environmentalism," in other words, should be seen as "the natural child of patriotism" (Milman 2021). The *New Ecology* movement was crafted under this framework (Neslen 2014). Similarly, as noted already, Le Pen's *144 Presidential*

Commitments proposed a number of sustainability measures, agricultural reforms, and energy transitions under the principle of "economic patriotism" (Le Pen 2017a). Juvin (2019) in turn, exhorted that major departures from recent government policies are needed: "only states in full possession of their territories can control, manage, and limit the activities of companies or their populations. Only nations that guarantee the borders and identity of their people can preserve their culture, their civilization, and the difference in their way of life."

Closely connected, RN firmly tied its pro-environmental repertoire to its vilification of domestic political elites. French politicians espousing globalized environmental actions could not be trusted. Le Pen accused Emmanuelle Cosse, the National Secretary of the Europe Ecology – The Greens *(Europe Ecologie Les Verts)* for France, of "promoting a profoundly anti-ecological model through the European Union and the absence of borders" (Martin 2014). Domestically, on environmental issues, RN warned of a "great false debate . . . completely locked down . . . [by] interminable lectures orchestrated by professor Macron" (La Tribune 2019). The result shall be that "the lower classes . . . will be the direct victims" (Bauduin 2017). RN mocked leading supporters of Paris's public transportation – which it considered a major contributor to urban air pollution – calling, for instance, Paris Mayor Anne Hidalgo "a great bobo ideologue" (Murer and Richermoz 2015) and Christophe Najdovski, the Mayor's deputy in charge of travel, someone who "lives out of touch, in an imaginary country where 'you don't need a car to get around Paris' because 'soft modes of transport (public transport, cycling or walking)' are enough" (de Saint-Just 2015). RN attacked laws supposedly protective of biodiversity but that restricted hunting activities as the "contempt of the government and the Greens for our fellow citizens in rural areas. . . . The 'ecologist' deputies. . . make their sectarianism triumph by destroying the hunting activity and its traditions" (Lherm 2015).

People-Centrism

The populist feature grounding RN's pro-environmental positions was its mandate to represent the people's will: Le Pen described herself as "the candidate of the people" working against the "evil" forces of globalization and elitism. "No French person, no part of France," she insisted, "must be forgotten" (Le Pen 2017a, p. 2). To support that, she promised that RN "want[s] every French citizen . . . to feel supported by the national community and by a careful and benevolent state. We want a strong state, we want a state that plays a strategic role in the economy – and who could blame us? For it is you the people who embody the state and what the state is, the instrument to fulfill your will" (Le Pen 2017b).

Given this, RN carried out this environmental vision in two distinct ways. The first was direct and explicit: it meant RN promising to convert people's will into environmental policies: RN's environmental stances should be seen as reflective of what people wanted. As d'Ornano stressed specifically when it came to the environment, "The New Ecology movement is based on national interest and patriotism. We have to be closer to our people and not against our country's interests" (Neslen 2014).

The 2021 *Counter-Project Referendum* on ecology signaled precisely this. It was to be seen in contrast to the government's top-down approach, not only the constitutional proposal set forth by president Macron during the same time but also earlier initiatives, such as Macron's *General State of Food*. As RN stated a few years earlier, "ordinary French people – individuals, associations – in short, sixty million consumers would like to have control over matters dealing with food – to improve its quality and cost, all in the service of relocated employment and respect of our environment." But the establishment had ignored them: "the first consultation, however, by the General Estates will take place without them – a fact deplored by various players, such as France Nature Environment and the small farming unions" (Collectif Nouvelle Ecologie 2017). What was needed was "a French Agricultural Policy" that would consult with and protect the interests of French farmers (ibid.). With this in mind, the introduction to the 2021 referendum (Rassemblement National 2021, p. 3) featured a photo of Le Pen smiling in a barn while gently holding a horse by its head. The initial page ends by noting that:

> This document therefore presents the 15 questions to be decided by the French, the legal text to organize this consultation, and the constitutional legal proposal aimed at translating the results of the popular vote on ecology. We believe it is urgent and necessary to enable all French people to take ownership of these fundamental issues for the future.

Earlier on that page, RN described the government's approach as a "punitive or ideological vision of ecology." RN's referendum, by contrast, sought to promote "a human ecology that puts the economy at the service of good living and health, but also at the service of preserving nature, biodiversity and our landscapes" (ibid.). Given this, the introductory language further stated that "every person has the right, within the conditions and limits defined by law . . . to participate in the formulation of public decisions with an impact on the environment." Accordingly, the document further stated that "Rassemblement National will table an ordinary bill organizing a national vote by universal suffrage on decisions affecting the environment" (ibid., p. 7). The message was unequivocal: RN wished to have the people be the drivers of the country's environmental policies, and would make itself the vehicle for the expression of the popular will.

This people-driven approach meant, as well, that RN would highlight the widespread benefits of its proposed policies for the people of France. After all, as reflective of the popular will, RN would surely pursue policies that benefited French citizens. A few years before the referendum, for instance, RN supported the nuclear sector as a positive not only for the environment but also for French citizens in a very immediate and practical sense: "the French," RN's 2014 amendment on the matter stated, "pay 40% less for electricity than the average European." It therefore seemed "inappropriate to turn away from a major asset for industry, the economy, employment, and the households of our country" (Assemblée Nationale 2014). Indeed, it is with in mind the "purchasing power of the French" and the "fight against energy poverty" that a house insulation program should be given budgetary priority. A new hydrogen sector should develop because it would be "our own energy." As for agriculture, the goal was to protect the values of small local farmers and thus "refuse factory-farms of the 1,000 cows type" (Assemblée Nationale 2014, Articles 131–137).

The second element of the vision was more abstract. It was the principle, as Juvin (2019) put it, of "human ecology." This was the idea that "authentic ecologists are those Europeans rooted in a region, a city, a village, who are from somewhere, and who want to remain at home . . ." and, again, that "ecology is a matter of local, singularities, and collective choices." Juvin argued that "the political ecology that we propose is first and foremost a human ecology, which places in the foreground the respect of peoples and their diversity, diversity of customs, beliefs and traditions, of political regimes, diversity of economic, legal and social systems." This necessarily translated into attention going to national borders and, crucially, a sense of place and, ultimately, the people who live there. Such romantic abstractions took on concrete manifestations whereby the common people were seen to drive and benefit from progressive environmental initiatives.

An example of this was the city of *Hénin-Beaumont* and the work of Christopher Szczurek, its deputy mayor and a member of RN's national board. The city deployed LED bulbs for all street and building lights, gave free trees to homeowners to shield against heat waves, and built a field dedicated to the "eco-grazing" of sheep (Onishi 2019). This was branded as a prominent example of RN's human ecology, whereby "for a long time, political parties took a hold of ecology and aimed it only at the bourgeois and well-off and now we see that the working class can also find something of real interest in it" (ibid.).

5 Right-Wing and Anti-Environment in the US

Trump's 'America First' Populism

Taking the Republican Party (also known as the Grand Old Party [GOP]) by storm, Donald Trump won the party's presidential primaries in summer of 2016 with 45% of the votes. Ted Cruz came a distant second, with 25% of the votes, followed by John Kasich with 14% and Marco Rubio with 11%. A few months later, Trump won the Electoral College with 304 votes compared to 224 for Hillary Clinton. It was a stunning victory that no one could have predicted a few years prior. Having never held public office, Trump performed like a true 'outsider,' vowing to 'Make America Great Again' by 'draining the swamp' in Washington D.C. and letting the people have a voice again.

For our purposes, Trump and the GOP serve as the representative case of a right-wing populist party that took anti-environmental positions. We begin by identifying those positions. We then examine Trump's anchoring of those stances in his people-centrism and anti-elitism. The stances offered him another platform from which to project his populism – in ways that were consonant with his ideological 'home,' his supporters' base, and the economic and political contexts in which he came to power.

Trump's Anti-Environmentalism

Trump rolled back over 100 pieces of major environmental rules governing a wide range of issues such as toxic chemicals and pollution, natural resource extraction, biodiversity, and global climate actions (Popovich et al. 2021). Under his leadership, the US withdrew from the 2016 *Paris Agreement*, one of the most significant global climate treaties of the past decades, which was agreed to under Obama's leadership (Friedman 2019a; Trump 2017a). He lifted the Obama-era control on methane, a significantly more potent greenhouse gas than carbon dioxide (Davenport 2020). He also loosened or eliminated various restrictions on coal – one of the dirtiest sources of energy – including those on mining and the operation of coal plants (Friedman 2019b) by replacing Obama's signature *Clean Power Plan* with the much weaker *Affordable Clean Energy Rule* (Irfan 2019). According to the Environmental

DOI: 10.4324/9781003423133-6

Protection Agency, the latter was estimated to lead to only a 1% reduction in greenhouse gas emissions from power plants (Gross 2020).

The Trump Administration also significantly curtailed previously established environmental review processes for infrastructural projects. Many of these had the potential to significantly impact the environment – for instance when it came to pipelines, drilling, and mining projects (Friedman 2021; Trump 2017b). Furthermore, Trump rolled back the long-standing legislative commitments to clean air and clean water kept by all presidents since the 1970s (Friedman and Davenport 2019). Fuel economy improvements for cars were reduced from 5% to 1.5% a year for models for years 2021 through 2026 (Gross 2020). Finally, Trump reduced the size of various national monuments by millions of acres (Gonzales et al. 2017).

Anchoring Work

These anti-environmental positions were not merely a part of a conservative agenda. Instead, Trump used them to advance his populist versions of anti-elitism and people-centrism. Those versions relied on a picture of the US as having experienced a terrible and long decline at the hands of a multifaceted elite intent on enriching itself while betraying true Americans (Campbell 2018). While there would follow countless expressions of his populist view, his 2016 *Wall Street Journal* opinion piece captured the essence of his perspective quite succinctly. As he wrote,

> I, for one, am not interested in defending a system that for decades has served the interest of political parties at the expense of the people. Members of the club – the consultants, the pollsters, the politicians, the pundits, and the special interests – grow rich and powerful while the American people grow poorer and more isolated. The only antidote to decades of ruinous rule by a small handful of elites is a bold infusion of popular will. On every major issue affecting this country, the people are right and the governing elite are wrong. The elites are wrong on taxes, on the size of government, on trade, on immigration, on foreign policy. What we are seeing now is not a proper use of the rules, but a flagrant abuse of the rules. Delegates are supposed to reflect the decisions of voters, but the system is being rigged by party operatives with 'double-agent' delegates who reject the decision of voters. (Trump 2016)

As he put forth this vision, Trump constructed various representations of the people based on sets of very carefully chosen identities designed for different contexts. The people could refer to American citizens when talking about anti-immigration, working-class Americans when denouncing big businesses and Washington elites, and white Americans when pushing back against the Black Lives Matter movement. In so doing, he showed that indeed "the people [in populist rhetoric] could be constructed with ethnic or political criteria, as a plural population or as a unitary actor" (Laclau 2005b, p. 48).

This fundamental perspective would be projected onto his environmental policies. These featured an attack on Obama-led Washington elites and the environmental policies they produced as fundamentally flawed and responsible for widespread job losses and industrial decline, and a concomitant promise to ordinary Americans that their economic problems would be solved with a nationalistic strategy of America's global dominance and energy sovereignty.

Before we analyze the relevant anchoring work, it will be useful to identify the key features of Trump's GOP leadership. Its basic ideology combined an aggressive form of conservative nationalism on economic policies, immigration, minority rights (for instance related to certain religious groups, ethnic groups, and the LGBTQIA+ community) and foreign policy with protectionist tendencies and withdrawals from international institutions and engagements (Staufer 2021). It also saw a move toward the deregulation of various economic sectors in line with neoliberal principles – though those same principles certainly did not apply to trade, where tariffs and other antagonistic measures were taken even when it came to Canada, Europe, and other close trading partners. Consistent with his populist anti-establishment message, Trump also moved to undermine a number of government agencies, departments, and judicial offices, while also supposedly boosting the defense and law-and-order budgets (Campbell 2023).

These measures were designed to please its base. Trump described his supporters as true Americans from the 'heartland' who had been betrayed by the nation's elites, harmed by unfair international competition, and eager to bring back America's 'greatness.' As various analyses showed over time, in practice this meant that his supporters – numbering many tens of millions – were fairly diverse. Yet, on the whole, the most dominant demographic was a combination of white, older, conservative and often religious, middle-class as well as working class, and non-college educated Americans who shared a cultural nostalgia for an older and to a fair extent imagined sort of US of limited ethnic diversity, less crime, more economic prosperity, less social liberalism, and stronger national presence on the world stage (Norris and Inglehart 2019; Pew Research Center 2018).

Trump's approach and electoral victory should be understood in the broader economic and political contexts of the time. The rise of China and economic globalization generated major trade imbalances for the US and led to the internal displacements of millions of workers who had worked in manufacturing-related jobs (Farley 2019). In tandem, the financial and debt crises of 2007–2008 ushered in many years of economic uncertainty, rising inequalities, and an ever-growing government debt. These economic developments led to an increase in political polarization, less effective government, and a sense among the public that politicians had abandoned the people (Campbell 2018). Hilary Clinton's presidential bid was further seen by many as yet another instance of the elites seeking to seize control at the expense of ordinary Americans. Trump presented himself as the answer to all of these problems. He promised that he alone could fix things. Millions of Americans believed him and he won the Presidency in 2016.

People-Centrism

Trump grounded his anti-environmental agendas as a key component of his mission to save the American people from decline and disaster. In his case, the 'people' referred primarily to two sorts of 'true' Americans, both closely associated with the economy: average Americans who deserved decent jobs and decent living standards under a strong American economy, and coal miners whose traditional way of living was taken away by pro-environmental policies and globalization.

First, then, Trump insisted that his dismantling of existing pro-environmental legislations should be seen as essential for the sort of economic development that would benefit the average American. Secure jobs in this regard were the cornerstones of his vision. As he put it, his "Make America Great Again" contained promises "made to American people during my campaign for President" that focused on "cutting job-killing regulation . . . bringing jobs, plants, and factories back into the United States at numbers which no one until this point thought even possible" (Trump 2017a). His anti-environmental agendas were an extension of this logic.

Hence, when Trump pulled the US out of the Obama Administration's major international climate accord, the *Paris Agreement*, he justified the move by appealing to the American people who were painted as victims of international treaties and environmental regulations. He repeated the claim that the *Paris Agreement* was a "job-killing" (Trump 2017a) deal for the average American in a string of statements, speeches, and rallies (see also Trump 2017c, 2017d, 2017e). To add credibility to his claims, he cited statistics. For instance, he argued that "compliance . . . could cost America as much as 2.7 million lost jobs by 2025 according to the National Economic Research Associates" and "according to this same study, by 2040 . . . the cost to the economy at this time would be close to $3 trillion in lost GDP and 6½ million industrial jobs, while households would have $7,000 less income and, in many cases, much worse than that" (Trump 2017a). Trump thus insisted that he could not let an international agreement "undermine our economy, hamstring our workers, weaken our sovereignty, impose unacceptable legal risk, and put us at a permanent disadvantage to the other countries of the world" (ibid.). As he promised, "As President, I can put no other consideration before the well-being of American citizens. . . . The Paris climate accord is . . . leaving American workers – who I love – and taxpayers to absorb the cost in terms of lost jobs, lower wages, shuttered factories, and vastly diminished economic production" (ibid.).

His deregulation of formerly protected natural resources was similarly presented as an effort to save and grow American jobs. During each year's *National Energy Awareness Month*, Trump's speeches inevitably contained promises of "unleashing our Nation's energy potential to drive robust job growth and expansion in every sector of our economy" (Trump 2017f; see also Trump 2018, 2019a, 2020a). When he challenged 14 states, led by California, that set more stringent tailpipe pollution standards than the federal government, he rallied auto workers by arguing that the federal deregulation he was proposing meant that "many more cars will be produced under the new and uniform standard, meaning significantly more JOBS, JOBS, JOBS!" (realdonaldtrump 2019). When Trump unilaterally weakened the *National Environmental Policy Act*, limiting public review of federal infrastructure projects to expedite permit approval processes for freeways, power plants, and pipelines, he taunted those projects as long overdue for the American people: they will "strengthen our economic platform . . . create millions of jobs, increase wages for American workers, and reduce the costs of goods and services for American families and consumers" (Trump 2017g).

In 2020, he would therefore reflect on his accomplishments for the American people during a speech dedicated to "rolling back environmental regulations:"

> Before I came into office, American workers were smothered by a merciless avalanche of wasteful and expensive and intrusive federal regulation. These oppressive burdensome mandates were a stealth tax on our people, slashing take home pay, suppressing innovation, surging the cost of goods, and shipping millions of American jobs overseas. Millions and millions and millions. It never ended. Nearly four years ago, we ended this regulatory assault on the American worker and we launched the most dramatic regulatory relief campaign in American history by far. No other administration has done anywhere near. (Trump 2020b)

Following these initial remarks, Trump then proceeded to list all the financial and other benefits that his environmental initiatives had procured for the American people: lower vehicle prices, "massive savings" on some energy bills, "historically low gasoline prices," consumer choice for home appliances (with dishwashers that could use much more water than before) and even traditional light bulbs ("incandescent light bulbs – I brought them back . . . they are cheaper and they are better . . . and they make you look so much better") (ibid.). As to jobs and work, again Trump linked his initiatives with major gains. As he put it, for instance,

> We stopped the egregious abuse of the Clean Water Act which extreme activists have used to shut down construction projects all across our country. When I signed that legislation I had many farmers and

construction people standing behind me. People that haven't cried since they were babies, some of them never even when they were a baby and they were crying. Many people were crying. We gave them back their life. They took away their land, they took away their rights, they took away their life. (ibid.)

Second, as part of these rhetorical efforts, workers in the energy sectors – and especially those in the shrinking coal-mining communities – became a focal point. Throughout his political career, coal miners became symbols of his romantic appeals to the old ways of life in America: honest people working hard to feed their families and fuel the American economy. They represented the 'heartland.' Trump tapped into the "nostalgia for preserving mining as a way of life and anger at outsiders disrupting their livelihoods and extractive moral economy" (Kojola 2019, p. 371). He thus skillfully mixed "environmental imaginaries and the social meanings of land, labor, and natural resources" (Kojola 2019, p. 377). Hence, reversing the fortunes of these workers who had suffered from the previous administration's 'War on Coal' became a central theme of his populism. As one of his senior administration officials responded to journalists in 2017 regarding this matter, "absolutely, I think he made a pledge to the coal industry, and he's going to do whatever he can to help those workers" (Trump 2017h).

Examples of this approach abound. At a rally in Nashville, for instance, Trump promised that "we're going to put our miners back to work. We're going to put our auto industry back to work. Already, because of this new business climate, we are creating jobs that are starting to pour back into our country like we haven't seen in many, many decades" (Trump 2017i). At a conservative conference in 2017, in turn, Trump announced that "we're preparing bold action to lift the restrictions on American energy, including shale, oil, natural gas, and beautiful clean coal, and we're going to put our miners back to work. Miners are going back to work. Miners are going back to work, folks. Sorry to tell you that, but they're going back to work" (Trump 2017j). A few years later, he praised coal miners in nearly mythological fashion: "I had people in my office – I had miners, and I had farmers, and I had builders building homes. And many of them were tough, strong men and women. And almost all of them were crying. They said, 'Sir, you've given our life back to us'" (Trump 2019b).

To these two dimensions of people-centrism, a third was added. This entailed the assertion that anti-environmentalism was necessary if America – that is, Americans – were to come first. The American people were entitled to determine their own future, without interference from foreign actors or interests. The *Paris Agreement* had therefore to be abandoned because it would inevitably lead to "future intrusions on the United States' sovereignty and massive future legal liability" (Trump 2017a). The US should also free itself from "reliance on the Organization of Petroleum Exporting Countries (OPEC) cartel" because "an energy dominant America is good for Americans – and good for the world" (Trump 2017f). This meant being no longer "beholden to foreign powers or domestic radicals. We are powering our Nation on our own terms" (Trump 2020a). Trump accordingly proceeded to open Alaska refuge's coastal plain for fossil fuel extraction (Fountain and Eder 2018). In parallel, of course, such energy independence also meant lower energy costs for Americans. At the 2020 World Economic Forum in Davos, Trump told those in attendance that his administration's deregulation efforts had saved American families an average of $2,500 a year in cheaper gasoline and electricity costs. By contrast, European consumers had suffered from "crippling" energy policies (Doyle and Farand 2020).

National pride thus also was at play. As Trump put it, "we're lucky. You go to places like China, they don't have oil and gas. They don't have it under their – they have to go buy it . . . But we have this unbelievable – the greatest in the world . . . now we're the number-one . . . energy producer in the world" (Trump 2019c). Hence, he justified his legislation relaxing environmental review processes for infrastructure investments by arguing that these would "strengthen our economy, enhance our competitiveness in world trade" (Trump 2017b). Such words, we can note here briefly, echoed the 'resource nationalism' of other populist leaders (see, for instance, Lyall and Valdivia 2019).

Anti-Elitism

Trump's anti-environmental positions were in parallel grounded in claims about the abandonment and betrayal felt by ordinary Americans as a result of the corrupt elites' pro-environmental policies. When it came to energy, for instance, he argued that "the previous administration waged a relentless war on American energy. . . . These radical plans would not make the world cleaner; they would just make and put Americans out of work, and they put them out of work rapidly" (Trump 2019d). He depicted the loss of energy jobs, especially for coal miners, as the result of the "relentless assault from the previous administration. . . . More than a third of all of the coal mining jobs had vanished" (Trump 2019b). The losses were the result of "federal regulations and bureaucrats [who] were working around the clock" to obstruct coal leases, drilling, mining, and energy infrastructure projects (ibid.).

Trump accordingly presented his anti-environmentalism as part of his battle against the selfish elites in the interests of the ordinary people. Hence, it became clear early on in his term that Trump was fixated on "dismantle[ing] the Obama Administration's climate change policies" (Carlson 2017). In this vein, Mick Mulvaney, the Director of US Office of Management and Budget under Trump, made it clear in 2017 that "we're not going to do some of the crazy stuff the previous administration did" in terms of climate policies (Trump 2017k). Trump's Secretary of Energy James Richard Perry set a similar tone in a cabinet meeting saying, "We're not going to be held hostage to some Executive order that was ill-thought-out" (Trump 2017l). Kathleen Hartnett White, whom Trump nominated in 2017 to head the White House Council on Environmental Quality, in turn had referred in 2016 to the belief in global warming as "paganism" for "the secular elites." "Global warming alarmists," she argued, "are misleading the public about carbon dioxide emissions," noting that carbon dioxide "makes life possible on earth and naturally fertilizes plant growth" (Anapol 2017).

Of course, the first blow went to the *Paris Agreement*, depicted as "simply the latest example of Washington entering into an agreement that disadvantages the United States" (Trump 2017a). It was the work of "two hundred and twenty-eight House Democrats" who "voted to put America back into the disastrous Paris climate accord." It was a bad deal not only for Americans, he noted: "How's that working out for Paris? How's that one working out for France? The yellow vests. They didn't like [it] . . . it hasn't been working out well" (Trump 2019e).

But Trump aggressively criticized many other policies of the Obama Administration. The Obama-led elites were accused of having colluded with foreign powers to undermine the American people's interests and to have "waged a relentless war on American energy. . . . They sought to punish our workers, our producers, and manufacturers with ineffective global agreements" (Trump 2019d). Revoking the *Waters of the United States Rule*, Trump branded himself as the protector of personal freedom and individual rights. In a statement, he claimed that "no longer will Federal bureaucrats be allowed to micromanage every public pond and drainage ditch on private land. They've taken away your rights. They took away your – they took away your heart" (Trump 2019b). Attacking Obama's *Clean Power Plan*, he claimed it "would have cost Americans nearly $40 billion a year and caused electricity prices to soar to double digits, while cutting coal production by almost 250 million tons" (ibid.). Turning to the Democrats' *Green New Deal* proposal, he again cited economic numbers and predicted job losses to back his claims: "Their plan is estimated to cost our economy nearly $100 trillion, a number unthinkable. . . [it will] kill millions of jobs; it will crush the dreams of the poorest Americans and disproportionately harm minority communities . . . we will defend American sovereignty, American prosperity, and we will defend American jobs" (Trump 2019d).

Importantly, the targets were not only federal-level regulations with national implications. Trump also applied the same logic to state-level matters. When shrinking the size of Utah's national monuments, Trump emphasized that Washington elites had infringed on the rights of Utahans. He declared that "the natural resources of Utah should not be controlled by a small handful of very distant bureaucrats located in Washington" (Turkewitz 2017). Republican Senator of Utah Mike Lee echoed this populist rhetoric by defending Trump's image as the president for the people of Utah and as someone who is "sympathetic to the fact that we've been mistreated . . . and I'm grateful that he is willing to correct it" (ibid.).

When it came to large-scale infrastructures, previous regulations mandated stringent environmental assessments to regulate projects that could pose serious harm to the environment and local ecology. Yet, Trump labeled these rules as unnecessary and a hindrance to the growth of national energy infrastructure as he argued that "for decades, special interest groups, bureaucrats, and radical environmental activists stymied the maintenance, repair, growth, and expansion of our Nation's energy infrastructure, preventing us from achieving energy independence" (Trump 2020a). Indeed, according to Trump, "the single biggest obstacle to building a modern transportation system has been mountains and mountains of bureaucratic red tape in Washington DC . . . Together we are reclaiming America's proud heritage of a nation of builders and a nation that can get things done" (Friedman 2021). The elites were portrayed as obstacles to the very heart of American nation-building. This stance on infrastructures reinforced Trump's populist appeal as a leader who could correct the wrongdoings of the elites – those "prophets of doom" (Doyle and Farand 2020) – that had alienated the people and endangered national interests.

Trump's speeches toward the end of his presidency gave him opportunities to revisit many of these same themes. Reflecting in 2020 on what a Biden presidency might bring in terms of the environment, he warned during remarks on the South Lawn of the White House about a socialist takeover by an administration so disconnected with everyday Americans that "thousands of companies, plants, factories would be closed. Under this dismal future energy would be unaffordable for the vast majority of Americans and the American dream would be sniffed out so quickly and replaced with a socialist disaster." By contrast, "Unlike the socialists," Trump reassured those assembled, "we believe in the rule of the people, not the rule of the unelected bureaucrats that don't know what they're doing" (Trump 2020b).

6 Left-Wing and Pro-Environment in Spain

Podemos's Bottom-Up Agenda

Podemos, a left-wing populist party, stole the spotlight as a disruptor of Spanish politics in the 2010s. Successful until 2021, Podemos won representation in the 2014 European Parliament elections (Errejón 2014). It secured around 20% of votes in the 2015 and 2016 regional and national elections (Rodríguez-Teruel et al. 2016). In 2020, it joined, albeit with reduced voters' support, the Spanish Socialist Workers' Party (*Partido Socialista Obrero Español* [PSOE]) in a coalition government (Rios 2019). Its successes dwindled in the subsequent years, with the party gaining only five seats (as part of the electoral platform Sumar) in the Congress of Deputies (the lower house of Parliament) and none in the Senate in the 2023 elections. Observers talked of fragmentation and decline (Ramalho 2023; Morel 2023).

Podemos offers a case of left-leaning populists with pro-environmental positions. We focus here on its years of prominence from the early 2010s to 2020. We analyze first those positions and then examine their anchoring in the party's populism. Like previous cases, those positions became material for Podemos to assert its vision of what the Spanish people needed and deserved and contrast that to the harms done by a corrupt political and business elite – in ways that were consonant with Podemos's ideological 'home,' its supporters' base, and the economic and political contexts in which Podemos had operated.

Podemos's Pro-Environmentalism

Podemos placed environmental issues at its platform's core. As the party stated in one of its communications, "Podemos has championed the fight against climate change politically in Spain since its inception, including in all its electoral programs proposals and key measures to combat it and curb its devastating effects" (Podemos 2019a). Critical of leading parties, it advocated for two major initiatives.

The first was the *Green New Deal (El New Deal Verde)*. Inspired by the 2019 *Green New Deal* proposal in the US Congress, it was an important element of its alliance with the PSOE for the 2019 elections campaign. With that

DOI: 10.4324/9781003423133-7

deal, Podemos promised, in the words of Txema Guijarro, a Podemos parliamentary representative, to "establish a number of strategic public companies. This will include a state investment bank so as to secure Spain's energy transition to 100 percent renewables over the next 20 years" (Gilmartin and Greene 2019). In addition, he added, "we are also proposing to create a public energy company, building on the great work at a municipal level in places like Barcelona where we have been governing with our allies in Barcelona en Comú. The creation of a public distribution company will be key in a context in which we have to undertake a profound transformation of all energy production" (ibid.).

Soon after, Podemos crafted its own and far more ambitious *Green Horizon Plan (Plan Horizonte Verde)*, calling for major emission-reduction targets. The plan, Podemos (2019a) stated, had a "fundamental objective that requires a massive transformation of our production system." Pablo Echenique, one of Podemos's Members of the European Parliament, then explained that "we want to reduce the electricity based on fossil fuels by half in a decade and reach 100% renewable energy production in 2040." In addition, "Podemos's ambitious proposal in the fight against climate change included a retrofitting of buildings for energy efficiency." This plan, Echenique added, "will allow for the reduction of up to 50% of electric bills and an average reduction of €400 per year per household." In so doing, the plan would align Spain with United Nations goals and those of the Paris Agreement.

At a cost of 2.5% of Spain's GDP – to be funded by public-private investments – the plan also called for cutting green-house emissions by 50% by 2030 and 90% by 2040, and integrated ecological and industrial policies. This, Echenique explained, would be at "a rate that is even above what the IPCC [the UN's Intergovernmental Panel on Climate Change] is currently asking for to stabilize the planet's temperature, which would place Spain in the place it deserves at the forefront of the fight against climate change and for renewable technologies" (ibid.).

Accompanying these two major initiatives were more targeted proposals. Among them was the party's intent to help small-scale farmers by providing them with sufficient financial and other guarantees to be able to continue their activities and compete against big agro-business – and, thereby, to ensure sustainability, the proper use of natural resources, and animal welfare. With this in mind, Podemos sought to influence the reform process of the EU's Common Agricultural Policy (CAP), since, it claimed, of all EU policies it is "likely that none influences more the environment and our daily lives" given that, among other things, the CAP commanded almost 40% of the EU's total budget (Podemos 2018). Its proposals included the prioritization of small-scale, local farming over large agro-business, more attention to sustainability, and an appreciation of the nexus between local agriculture and the environmental, social, and economic wellbeing of communities.

Anchoring Work

Podemos was from its start fundamentally populist. Led by political scientist Pablo Iglesias and his explicit embrace of populism (Hancox 2015), Podemos branded itself as serving "popular unity and citizenship" to reclaim the sovereignty that Spaniards lost to the "oligarchic 'caste'" (Errejón 2014; Gilmartin and Greene 2019) that had for too long taken control of Spain's economic and political systems. These included, above all, career politicians of the main political parties and the country's big business elites – in banking, energy, and other sectors. Podemos thus spoke to the youth especially and called for direct citizens' participation in politics. Iglesias stressed that the party is about "citizens doing politics. If the citizens don't get involved in politics, others will. And that opens the door to them robbing you of democracy, your rights and your wallet" (Kassam 2014). But Podemos also spoke to the unemployed more generally, workers, small-scale business owners, and more broadly the Spanish people who, it felt, had been ignored and excluded from the country's economy and political system.

Podemos branded itself not only as a party that stood up and advocated for ordinary citizens' rights, but also one, according to Íñigo Errejón, Podemos's campaign director, that felt that "we don't want to structure ourselves in the same closed off way. . . . We're a citizen force, made up of people who got together and ran an electoral campaign practically without any money" (ibid.). Hence, As Guijarro put it, "the fundamental thing that differentiates us from the other forces . . . is a participatory politics where we appeal to a certain kind of people power. That doesn't just mean canvassing, debating, and putting up posters. It's also a matter of basing ourselves on mass mobilization and small donations" (Gilmartin and Greene 2019). Thus, Podemos pitched itself as truly 'bottom-up:' as in effect a social movement that acquired political characteristics.

Practical demonstrations of this abounded. Podemos opened its 2014 European Parliament elections' primaries to anyone, attracting 33,000 voters (ibid.). A cornerstone of its projects were in turn the *indignado*-style 'circles,' or local assemblies. These were meant to invite local communities to meet, debate, and vote (Tremlett 2015). Errejón (2014) described them as signaling "the existence of a people not represented by the dominant political castes, and which is beyond left and right metaphors." In another instance, ahead of the 2014 elections, Podemos hand-delivered its campaign letter to mailboxes. In it, Iglesias wrote that

This letter did not reach you by post, because mailing a letter like this all over the country costs over 2 million Euros. Ask the parties who sent you an election letter by post where they got the money to do so and in exchange for what. We don't ask for favors from bankers or corrupt [politicians] and we publish all our accounts on the web. If you are reading this it is because someone who lives near you wants to change things for real. (Fominaya 2014)

Podemos projected these populist standpoints onto environmental stances. Those stances became vehicles to express its populism. They were presented as originating with the people in mind, and thus as dismantling the established interests. Before we examine such anchoring work, as with the other case studies we should consider relevant key factors pertinent to Podemos.

Ideologically, Podemos was fundamentally suspicious of capitalism and neoliberalism. In the words of Iglesias, it viewed inequality as the "primary menace," along with corruption, privatization, and parasitic institutions (Wong 2018). Podemos's priorities made it a far-left political party that was critical not only of right-leaning parties but also of center-left ones. Indeed, in 2019, ahead of national elections, Iglesias campaigned by reminding voters that the PSOE under the leadership of Pedro Sánchez "had not made good on his promises to impose a bank tax, overturn neoliberal labor reforms, or release the names of those involved in a controversial tax amnesty" (Gilmartin and Greene 2019). Iglesias accused the PSOE of being able and willing to align itself with right-wing parties and thereby undermine workers' security, democracy, and genuine sovereignty (Wong 2018). While Podemos was not shy to describe itself as 'anti-capitalist,' the same could obviously not be said of the PSOE.

Podemos's proposals accordingly included, in the words of Guijarro, universal infant education up to three years, "a thirty-four hour work week and a guaranteed grant for up to six months – equivalent to the monthly minimum wage – for women who have suffered gender violence. These measures aim to put the welfare and rights of women and families above that of capital" (Gilmartin and Greene 2019). Feminism became a central element of this platform – with many informational and other videos on its YouTube channel[1] dedicated to gender equality and women's rights. Podemos also proposed improvements to old age pensions. All the while, it opposed the financial sector because it was "the enemy of human aspiration" (Wong 2018).

Podemos's supporter base was diverse. The young and other Spaniards who were worried about economic insecurities, political corruption, and true democratic representation made up its core – as analyses of the 2014 elections showed. Disgruntled leftist voters left the PSOE to support Podemos. Among the voters were also those who had never voted before (Fominaya 2014). Thematically, those who were concerned about corruption and did not trust the two traditional main parties – the social democratic PSOE and the conservative Populist Party *(Partido Popular* [PP]) – seemed especially likely to vote for Podemos (Orriols and Cordero 2016).

Podemos's impressive rise in the world of Spanish politics should be seen in very specific economic and political contexts. Economically, though Spain had seen relatively strong growth compared to some other European countries, it was recovering from the 2007–2008 financial crisis, years of austerity programs (supported by both the PSOE and the conservative PP), and anger about the use of public money to socialize banks' debts

(Orriols and Cordero 2016; Fominaya 2014). Some of the highest unemployment levels in Europe meant that ordinary Spaniards struggled. In 2015, when reflecting on Podemos's sudden and meteoric rise, an article in *The Guardian* noted that "one-third of the labour force is either jobless or earns less than the minimum annual salary of €9,080" (Tremlett 2015). Distrust of the PSOE and PP, and their 80-year-old deadlock on politics, was high. Many in the country, according to observers, were ready for a new sort of political language (Fominaya 2014).

People-Centrism

With the above in mind, we can begin by noting that Podemos squarely presented its environmentalism as fundamentally associated with the people. Its plans came from the people, depended on the people, and were for the people. Its language made clear that it was impossible to think of the environment as something separate from the people, or as distinct from Podemos's commitment to the Spanish people.

First, then, Podemos insisted that its positions came *from* the people – especially young ones, who were its core base. When announcing its *Green Horizon Plan*, Echenique claimed that "Podemos supports the mobilization of young people for the climate and we thank them for saying that we will only stop change if we make profound reforms of the economic model" (Podemos 2019a). In reference to the *Green New Deal*, Iglesias in turn stated, "the young people who have come out onto the street telling us we do not have two planets" are a major inspiration for the party's mobilization (Gilmartin and Greene 2019). Podemos's YouTube channel broadcasted similar messages. In a campaign video for their *Green New Deal*, for example, a young woman announced that "students from all over the world are mobilizing and finding their own ways of doing politics to demand real and courageous actions against climate change. . . . Hundreds of thousands of young people say emphatically that if the planet was a bank, we would have already rescued it" (Podemos 2019b). The video ends with "We [the youth] are the ones who will have to live that future. If we want, we can" (ibid.).

The young were not the only constituency from the people driving Podemos's policies. In a 2018 video titled *The Field Is not a Factory (El Campo no Es una Fábrica)* (Podemos 2018) and produced ahead of EU-level negotiations over the CAP, Podemos focused on small-scale farmers and ranchers and their calls for agricultural reform, sustainability, and the protection of lands. The video begins with Podemos deputies and party members articulating the party's position and answering – with idyllic backgrounds featuring fields, sheep, farmland, and other pastoral scenes – the question that appears on the screen: "What do we want?" But soon the speakers become people who have – at first – no identified names or titles. They stand by irrigated fields, rolling hills, and orchards. The viewer gradually understands that these are small-scale farmers and ranchers. They appear after the question "What Do We Propose?" flashes on the screen, with the background featuring a small village nestled in a forest, with its church's bell tower visible and ringing.

One farmer, standing in front of an orchard where three people can be seen picking fruits from a tree, answers that what they want is "to prioritize farms with fewer than 30 hectares." Another, surrounded by goats in a snowy valley, states that "we propose to help sustainable agricultural farms that maintain biodiversity and support the social and economic fabric of depopulated areas," adding that "ecological agriculture" is what needs help. Yet a third, with presumably behind him his son and tilled fields, says that "we propose to increase complementary pay for young farmers and ranchers." And another, standing by another orchard where workers can be seen collecting fruits, states that he wishes to make aid "conditional on compliance with labor rights and basic sanitary and environmental norms." The viewer then hears from a rancher, who asks that aid for cattle farming should be given with in mind "the particularities of our woody and Mediterranean pastures." A peaceful image of a wooden dock with two small boats and birds chirping follows. The message is clear: Podemos is the voice of the people.

Second, people-centrism meant reliance *on* the people to make progress. When announcing the *Green Horizon Plan*, Podemos (2019a), for instance, stressed that "the implementation of these measures will require an unprecedented mobilization of all the productive and intellectual energies of our country." This would necessarily draw from the resources of all Spaniards: it "is a participatory politics where we appeal to a certain kind of people power . . . basing ourselves on mass mobilization" (Gilmartin and Greene 2019). Promotional materials like the video *The Field Is not a Factory* drew directly from the people to state what the party was about. Podemos had little organizational resources and relied, in principle and in all its initiatives, on thousands of supporters to carry out its mission (Tremlett 2015).

Third, people-centrism meant policies *for* the people. As Echenique claimed, "you cannot take care of the environment without taking care of people first" (Podemos 2019a). Podemos promised that sustainability's costs would not fall disproportionately onto common citizens. As *Unidas Podemos* – the coalition that Podemos joined for the 2016 general elections – asserted, "the cost of an ecological transition cannot be borne by those who are most affected. The cost has to be for those who have polluted the most. That is why we are talking about a change in the production model . . . because it has to decrease from above and not from below" (Gallego 2019).

Relatedly, Podemos turned its attention to jobs. Youth unemployment rate in Spain had been among the highest in Europe. Guijarro stated that "the necessity of confronting climate change is also an opportunity to create quality employment in a country where there is still a 14 percent unemployment rate." Referring to the creation of the envisioned public energy company, public distribution company, and related measures, he stressed that they "imply a program of mass public employment, the likes of which have never really been seen in Spain before. We are talking about the creation of hundreds of thousands of new jobs" (Gilmartin and Greene 2019).

Similarly, Podemos assured its base of young supporters that the *Green New Deal*'s promised transition of energy companies' ownership from private to public via the creation of a national company would "generate quality jobs, reduce inequalities, and take care of the planet as a priority" (Podemos 2019b). According to Pablo Echenique – not only a Member of the European Parliament for Podemos during 2014–2015 but also a representative in the country's Congress of Deputies in 2019 – the *Green New Deal* aimed "to create hundreds of quality jobs, increase innovation, recover migrated talent, and start a path to compete at the top in the value-added industry so as to compete with countries like Germany or Japan, and not compete in terms of job insecurity" (Podemos 2019a).

Podemos used similar rhetoric when it came to the *Green Horizon Plan*. It reassured citizens, for instance, stating that "the creation of two jobs for each job that is lost will be guaranteed by law." In the same vein, when it came to the challenge of fighting wildfires, Podemos committed itself to "improving the working conditions of professionals and increasing the size of the workforce" (ibid.).

Anti-Elitism

Podemos's environmentalism was concomitantly anchored in its disdain for the elite. "The 'caste' was a diffuse term that could include politicians, bankers, speculators, and any other privileged group; a floating signifier to which anyone . . . could turn to express their indignation against the establishment" (Sola and Rendueles 2018, p. 104). The 'oligarchic caste' was depicted as being responsible for the hijacking of sovereignty and democracy (Errejón 2014). Iglesias made clear that it should be opposed: "look, those people are your enemies" (Tremlett 2015) and they are the "enemies of Spain" (Gilmartin and Greene 2019).

The elites' actions caused the environmental crisis. This, often, was also presented as ultimately hurting the people too – for the environment and the people should always be seen as closely related. "Finance is against democracy," Iglesias stated in an interview with *The Nation*, and "finance is against the people and the environment" (Wong 2018). Hence, regarding forest fires, for instance, Podemos claimed that "economic interests exert a great influence on the forest land: they socialize the environmental losses and impacts and privatize the benefits, leaving aside the majority interest of the citizenry." It pointed the finger at the "privatization and outsourcing of fire prevention and services," which themselves "give rise to an economic network of interests that must be monitored very scrupulously" (Podemos Environmental Area 2017). Selfish actors stood to benefit from the fire crisis.

And their behavior will never change. As Podemos's *Green New Deal* campaign video asserted, "the great fortunes of the banks, the vulture funds and the larger energy companies have seen their profits multiply." They have no incentives to change. Indeed, the same point applies to anyone dependent on those actors. As the video states: "Those who have debts and dealings with banks, utilities or funds cannot, even if they wanted to, make these changes a reality." What is needed is therefore to have "hands free" from those entanglements (Podemos 2019b). Podemos accordingly proposed various policies to preserve forest "ecosystems and the sustainable natural landscape . . . the hallmarks of the rural environment" (Podemos Environmental Area 2017). It also made promises of forest management based on the needs of rural populations who felt left behind by private interests and distant governing bodies.

In this spirit, in the *Green Horizon Plan* Podemos advanced two anti-elitist solutions: "the prohibition of revolving doors between public officials and the boards of directors" and, as already mentioned, "the creation of a public energy company" (Gallego 2019). Such changes were necessary: Iglesias had exposed former political leaders who were members of energy corporations' boards of directors (as with *Naturgy*, *Abengoa*, and *Enagas*). He argued that "if these companies buy former ministers and former presidents, it is impossible to face the challenges of climate change" (ibid.). Moreover, their greed translated into 'energy poverty' for the common people: "the profit margin of the large Spanish electricity companies (for their business in Spain) practically doubles that of their European counterpart: what we could call 'extra profits' . . . amount to €9,400 million. This money has come out of the consumer's pocket" (Podemos 2016).

Iglesias promised to "put in 'order' the oligopoly of the private sector" with public energy companies and "the installation of renewable energies . . . to guarantee that no one suffers from energy poverty" (Gallego 2019). Nationalization would make "access to energy, like access to housing or education . . . a citizen's right" (Podemos 2016). "This," Guijarron noted, "will obviously come into conflict . . . with the interests of the existing energy giants. The energy market in Spain is really a cartel, with some of the highest prices in Europe. And so we are also aiming to challenge this capture of the market by establishing such a national company" (Gilmartin and Greene 2019). Only "when we have true equality and greater democracy," stated Iglesias, "we will be able to confront the despotic power of corporations, transition away from an economy based on fossil fuels, and guarantee a sustainable economy that will ensure the survival of future life on this planet" (Wong 2018).

The party's official statement for *World Environment Day* in 2015 perhaps best captured its anti-elitist anchoring. Its key passages are worth reporting here:

> Governments, by kidnapping institutions, protect an unsustainable production model that is causing the depletion of natural resources, energy geodependence and the greatest environmental problem facing Humanity: Climate Change. . . . The kidnapping by public administrations that should

watch over nature and make Spain progress towards sustainability has launched partisan policies favoring a privileged minority while resources are depleted, our rivers and mountains are polluted and our unique species perish. . . . We are faced with the political responsibility of abandoning any policy that does not assume that there is only one planet and that it is finite. (Podemos 2015)

As what we have discussed so far suggests, much of Podemos's attention, when it came to its anti-elitism and its environmental stances, focused on domestic actors – at least implicitly. But of course, like the RN in France, Podemos also presented its environmentalism as part of its populist reactions to international elites. Among the targets, as noted earlier, were EU bureaucrats and the CAP. That policy was depicted as catering to large-scale agricultural businesses, and its logic as part of a capitalist profit-making drive totally removed from the needs of small farmers, who in fact were the ones who could provide genuine and healthy food products. *The Field Is not a Factory* thus featured direct attacks on the CAP and the presumed interests driving it. One farmer asks that there be a list of activities unrelated to farming (such as railways and airports) that should stop receiving funding from the CAP. Earlier in the video a Podemos delegate described the lofty and abstract environmental, biodiversity, and agricultural goals of the CAP before noting that:

The reality, though, is that the agrifood system that the CAP promotes is designed to benefit above all the large owners and industrial agriculture – the most intensive and unsustainable. The field is turning into a factory focused exclusively on increased production, while the CAP marginalizes the farmers and ranchers that do the best things . . . those small and middle farmers that represent the social model of Mediterranean agriculture. (Podemos 2018)

Indeed, Podemos argued, the elite's international interests interlocked with those of the domestic elites with the resulting harms suffered by the true, genuine people of the country.

Note

1 www.youtube.com/@ahora_podemos/videos

7 Left-Wing and Anti-Environment in Venezuela

Chávez's and Maduro's Anti-Capitalist Resource Nationalism

This chapter examines Venezuela's Socialist populist regime under Hugo Chávez and Nicolás Maduro since 1999. Chávez led the country with the support of the Socialist Fifth Republic Movement *(Movimiento Quinta República)* until 2007, and then founded the United Socialist Party of Venezuela (*Partido Socialista Unido de Venezuela* [PSUV]), which would later support Maduro as Venezuela's leader. After Chávez's death, Maduro continued the same policies that Chávez had pursued, despite considerable domestic and international resistance.

Chávez and Maduro represent a case of left-leaning populists who adopted anti-environmental stances. As with the other case studies, we analyze first those positions and then examine their anchoring in the party's populism. As we shall see, it is indeed impossible to separate the regime's environmental positions from its purported socialist drive to serve and offer the Venezuelan *'pueblo'* a rebirth of sorts after decades of abuses and appropriations of the country's vast natural resources by national and international elites.

The Socialist Party's Anti-Environmentalism

As is well known, Venezuela depended heavily on the extraction of natural resources. The state-owned oil company Petróleos de Venezuela S.A. (PDVSA) was a major asset (Baena 2019; Berg 2021; Hellinger 2016, 2021; Wiseman and Béland 2010). Oil, mostly taken from the Orinoco Oil Belt *(Faja Petrolífera del Orinoco)*, accounted for 95% of the country's export earnings, and over half of the federal budget as of 2012. Chávez's *Sowing the Oil Crop Plan* (*Plan Siembra Petrolera*) aimed to produce four million barrels of oil a day by 2014 and ten million by 2030 (Heinrich Boell Foundation 2012). The entire economic system and government budgets were deeply reliant on such sources of income.

Once in power, Chávez and later Maduro took broadly anti-environmental positions reflective of the country's deep dependence on oil and mineral extraction. The regime sought to increase production and expand extractivist operations while reducing regulatory constraints to generate greater profit.

DOI: 10.4324/9781003423133-8

This was seen as essential to support Chávez's varied spending programs and in turn secure electoral support at key junctures (Heinrich Boell Foundation 2012). Attention went especially to expanding oil and natural gas extraction, with relatively little concern for the environmental damages caused. As the Center for Strategic & International Studies wrote when reflecting on the Chávez and Maduro years, "the regime in Caracas has presided over a significant decline in environmental standards" (Berg 2021).

Between 2010 and 2016 PDVSA reported, for instance, more than 46,000 oil spills. Part of the response was the government's announcement that it would actually stop reporting spills starting in 2016 (Berg 2021). In 2021, an oil tank at Punta Cardón in Falcón State leaked 3.6 million liters of gasoline over nine days through a crack in its base. The leak was attributed to a lack of maintenance since 2016 as well as failing to take action when the leak was first detected. The year prior should have served as a warning, when the El Palito refinery leaked over 20,000 barrels of oil into the water that spread to the protected Morrocoy National Park. These and other damages resulted from a "disturbing pattern: the Venezuelan regime's desire to reopen refineries as soon as possible exacerbates the response, prevents lessons learned, and makes future catastrophes more likely to occur" (ibid.). As to natural gas, Venezuela ranked among the top six countries in the world for gas flaring – the combustion of natural gas by-products that could be captured and utilized but are instead burnt off – with a resulting release of a considerable amount of methane into the atmosphere (ibid.).

When reacting to international sanctions on oil exports, Maduro in turn shifted his extractive focus to expand mining in the Orinoco Mining Arc *(Arco Minero del Orinoco)*. This opened up to 112,000 square kilometers of the Amazon rainforest – some of the most biodiverse areas of the entire rainforest that borders Canaima National Park, a UNESCO World Heritage Site – for mining. It contained proven reserves of thousands and millions of tons of gold, diamonds, iron, bauxite, copper, and coltan (Ebus 2018; Notilogía 2016; Rendon et al. 2020). No environmental impact assessment in the region was carried out despite being mandated by law (Ebus 2018). On the contrary, the Maduro regime reportedly used the state security apparatus to help rampant criminal mining groups extract, process, and sell minerals (Rendon et al. 2020).

Essentially all of these initiatives were consistent with the grand objectives for the country as set out in PSUV's comprehensive *Law of the Homeland Plan: Second Socialist Plan for the Economic and Social Development of the Nation 2013–2019 (Ley del Plan de la Patria: Segundo Plan Socialista de Desarrollo Económico y Social de la Nación 2013–2019* [LHP]). The LHP, while including some language about ecological responsibility and the harmonious use of natural resources, laid out a long list of detailed objectives calling for the expansion of the state's profitable oil and mining operations. These included extraction projects, production expansion, development of new and existing sources of energy (from natural gas to oil), new oil refineries, and more drilling operations (Grand Objective No. 3 of the LHP offered in this regard a detailed and ambitious list). As might be expected, these developments set off alarm bells among foreign observers. As early as 2007, in fact, the EU had warned about the "continued difficulties in relation to the country's environmental performance and achievements. Particular challenges include deforestation, desertification, a reduction in biodiversity, insufficient management of waste and pollution caused by industry, agriculture, and mining areas" (European Commission 2007, p. 13). But little response obviously came from the Venezuelan government. Despite occasional mentions of climate change and environmental crises, its primary stances focused on the sustained and expanding exploitation of the country's natural resources.

Anchoring Work

These anti-environmental stances did not stand separate from Chávez's and Maduro's populist rhetoric. They were instead deeply rooted in their anti-elitism and people-centrism. These emphasized an anti-imperialist agenda and grievances against the exploitative nature of international capitalism and its supporters which, in turn, should be countered with a drive for self-sufficiency and poverty alleviation that would benefit all Venezuelans. Chavismo projected an "antagonistic duality" where a "rancid oligarchy" had for a long time exploited "*el pueblo*" (Roberts 2012, p. 136). The time had come to claim the country's riches back for the people.

To fully understand this, we should first consider some basic factors pertinent to the regime. In ideological terms, Chávez positioned himself as the true representative of the people – indeed, almost a missionary of sorts, the people's "humble soldier who will only do what you [the people] will say" (Hawkins 2009, p. 1040) – by campaigning for Socialist programs and a Marxist-informed Bolivarian revolution centered on massive social spending from oil revenues, the nationalization of key industries, and a direct form of democracy "based on plebiscitarian expressions of popular sovereignty and grassroots participation in community organizations and self-governing structures" (Roberts 2012, p. 138; see also Farnsworth 2021). His redistributive politics positioned him squarely against most of the business community.

Maduro, as the handpicked successor for Chávez, followed in his footsteps and continued Chavismo as he asserted that "I am doing nothing else but fulfilling the mission entrusted to me by Comandante President Hugo Chávez Frías as I have been doing and as I will do out of love for his person and his work" (Venezuela 2013, p. 5). Aside from his dubious electoral victory after Chávez's death and fraud allegations overshadowing subsequent elections, Maduro clung to power as Chávez himself had done: with the appeal and promises of a populist rhetoric. As he put it to all Venezuelans, "I, Nicolás

Maduro Moros, am a genuinely and profoundly democratic president" (Phillips 2019).

Socialism at home was accompanied by the demonization of the domestic elites, who for long had sought to enrich themselves, and of the US as the 'imperialistic neighbor' threatening Venezuelan freedom and independence, especially after "Washington's thinly veiled support for the military coup that briefly removed him [Chávez] from office in April 2002" (Roberts 2012, p. 145–146). Chávez claimed that the US was attempting to subject Venezuela to political and economic neocolonialism. As he stated it in his 2006 campaign's closing speech, he and Venezuela as a whole were in a "cosmic" struggle against evil:

> Let no one forget that we are confronting the Devil himself. Sunday, 3 December at the ballot box. We will confront the imperialist government of the United States of North America [sic] – that is our real adversary, not these has-beens here, these lackeys of imperialism. . . . Because you are not going to reelect Chávez really, you are going to reelect yourselves, the people will reelect the people. Chávez is nothing but an instrument of the people. (Hawkins 2009, p. 1040–1041)

This theme would also be central to Maduro's core perspective – extending it, as Chávez himself had done – to Europe and beyond. As Maduro exhorted in a speech to fellow Chavistas and international allies at the start of his second term in 2019:

> Stop, Europe. . . . Don't come again with your old colonialism. Don't come again with your old aggression. Don't come again, old Europe, with your old racism. There's been enough enslavement – the looting that you subjected us to for 500 years. . . . We are a true, profound, popular, and revolutionary democracy . . . not a democracy of the elites . . . of super-millionaires who go into power to enrich their economic group and to rob the people. (Phillips 2019)

Regarding the regime's supporters, Chávez sought to reach the common people: honest, hardworking Venezuelans of all backgrounds who had suffered from the injustices of foreign capitalist interests. Farmers, public sector workers, laborers, Indigenous communities, and everyday citizens seeking an end to poverty and widespread redistribution of wealth were thus in principle his base. The early years of the regime saw a largesse of spending and significant improvements in many sectors of society. As a result, support for the regime was diverse and broad, although concentrated among the lower classes (Roberts 2012). At the same time, it also included those who, put in leadership positions, could benefit significantly and often illicitly from the new politics.

All this was unfolding in rather specific economic and political contexts that featured a fossil-fuel driven developing economy, a struggling working class, and a single-party regime that systematically repressed any meaningful opposition. The timing of Chávez's run for President and election had proven perfect. Shortly after taking office in 1999, the price of oil rose significantly. With billions of dollars of oil revenues unexpectedly available, the government spent generously on health care, infrastructure, wages, and a ballooning public sector (Farnsworth 2021). Popular support stayed high in the early years, and Chávez used this positive momentum to build international alliances in Latin America and establish or promote a number of hemispheric international organizations, such as the Bank of the South *(Banco del Sur)* and the South American Defense Council.

Conditions in the country eventually worsened with time, as sanctions and lower commodity prices deprived the country of essential access to markets and revenues. As poverty spread, emigration increased. While those elements of the political and economic elites that were benefiting from the regime continued to express support, the state relied increasingly on repression and anti-democratic strategies to squash any dissent.

Anti-Elitism

Zúquete (2008, p. 92) characterized Chavismo as a form of "missionary politics" in which a charismatic leader "leads a chosen people gathered into a moral community struggling against all-powerful and conspiratorial enemies, and engaged in a mission toward redemption and salvation." When it came to the environment, this meant casting the regime's appropriation and exploitation of the country's extractive resources as a powerful expression of the rejection of the elites who until then had, according to Chávez and later Maduro, used the same resources for their own enrichment. The regime's extractive policies were presented, in other words, as a way of cleansing the industry of the elites' moral and practical corruption. As Sagarzazu and Thies (2019, p. 208) wrote, Chávez claimed that those elites' "extract[ion of] the country's resources for their own benefit, and continued acceptance of the political and economic oppression of U.S. imperialism" had ensured "political and economic stagnation" and "the loss of economic sovereignty." What was needed in response was 'oil populism:' the rejection of those elites combined with the assertion of extractive nationalism for national rebirth.

This meant then, first, the casting of the elites as selfish and exploitative. These included painting the managers and owners of the country's energy resources as pillagers. Chávez denounced PDVSA's managers, for instance, as part of an "exploitative international ruling elite. . . [the] *petroleum elite*, which for years managed the enterprise that belongs to all Venezuelans, has now revealed its mask. Behind an alleged meritocracy there was always hidden a deep anti-national and anti-Venezuelan sentiment" (Agence France

Press 2002 as cited in Wiseman and Béland 2010, p. 154). This was so even though PDVSA had been in principle nationalized in the 1970s. Chávez accused those in control of PDVSA of enriching themselves, in conjunction with their foreign affiliates and operators – and proceeded to take action to change its leadership and rules of operation (Hellinger 2016). But the elites also included those on the international stage who set the rules around energy and climate policy. Claudia Salerno (2012), for instance, Venezuela's top negotiator at the *2012 Doha Climate Change Conference* (COP 18), voiced Venezuela's objections to pro-environmental carbon trading by criticizing it as a global capitalist scheme. It created "mechanisms to take profit of a certain kind of pollution." Venezuela would accordingly not subscribe to it because it would hamper the country's ability to profit from its industries.

The resulting second step was therefore depiction of the regime's plans related to natural resources and extraction as a way to fix, or redress, the elite's wrongful actions. For instance, in PSUV's comprehensive LHP, objective II was "to continue building the Bolivarian socialism of the 21st century in Venezuela as an alternative to the destructive and savage system of capitalism" (Venezuela 2013, p. 4). This, of course, meant oil extraction achieved by "transcending the capitalist oil rentier model towards the socialist productive economic model, based on the development of the productive forces" (Venezuela 2013, p. 11). Maduro would himself repeatedly claim that the country was taking steps to boost its oil production – often by setting impossible targets. During his annual speech to Congress in 2021, for instance, he claimed, without specifying any details, that "we are prepared for a productive recovery and our goal is to reach 1.5 million bpd to be sold to the world thanks to new production, financing and marketing mechanisms." He explained this would be in part possible because "oil workers have found themselves on top to ensure production, reduction of extraction costs and new ways of financing" (Palmigiani 2021). This contrasted with OPEC's monthly bulletin at the time, which reported Venezuela producing an average of 557,000 bpd in 2020 – "the lowest in more than 70 years" (ibid.). Maduro applied the same logic to the state's control and expansion of the mining industry. He and Minister of Ecological Mining Development Robert Mirabal saw for example gold production in the Orinoco Mining Arc as a symbol of national victory in the "economic war" against foreign sanctions and of the success of the Venezuelan "productive model" (Rosales 2017, p. 132–133).

In a separate approach, Chávez and Maduro sought to demonize the US and the EU, who had put sanctions against Venezuela to prevent it from accessing world markets, as seeking to stifle the country's ability to survive by exploiting its natural resources. The regime was, in other words, doing all it could to benefit Venezuela by developing its most valuable industries, but foreign actors were sabotaging its efforts. As Maduro argued after taking power, "If Venezuela can't produce oil and sell it, can't produce and sell its gold, can't produce and sell its bauxite, can't produce iron, etcetera, and can't earn revenue in the international market," it will have no future. Venezuela could not, to start, pay its debts: "How is it supposed to pay the holders of Venezuelan bonds?," Maduro asked. He concluded that "this world has to change. This situation has to change" (Schatzker et al. 2021). The US sanctions (most significantly on oil exports) imposed on pro-Maduro parties and businesses – for Maduro's violation of democratic principles and human rights – were therefore characterized by Maduro as "assault," "financial persecution," and "sabotage" (Palmigiani 2021) "by the North American empire" (Albaciudad. org 2020). In response, Maduro painted himself as a strongman defending Venezuela against "an illegal embargo . . . aggression against our government. We are resisting this criminal, inhuman aggression . . . [and] fighting for peace, for our homeland, for our region, for humanity" (United Nations 2020).

Years before, as he sought to take full control of PDVSA, Chávez had used similar language when he "redefined [its role] in line with the broader national interest" (Buxton 2003, p. 125) by promising to favor local capital over foreign one (Parker 2005, p. 45). "PDVSA belongs to all Venezuelans," he stressed (Agence France Presse 2002 as cited in Wiseman and Béland 2010, p. 154). Similarly, when it came to the LHP, its "fourth major historic objective [was] to move forward in the search for a multi-centric and pluripolar world, without imperial domination and with unrestricted respect for the self-determination of peoples" (Venezuela 2013, p. 4). This was translated into initiatives such as "Policy 27. Oil Sovereignty," whose aim was "to reduce the economic, industrial and technological dependence of the national oil industry" and "to strengthen Full Oil Sovereignty." Interestingly, an analysis of Chávez's weekly *Aló Presidente* talk shows over the years (of which there were 378 between 1999 and 2012) showed that his propensity to engage in anti-imperialist language was directly related to the price of oil. When that price was high, he engaged in it. When it was low, he stopped doing so (Sagarzazu and Thies 2019).

People-Centrism

People-centrism became the justifying centerpiece for the state's profitable oil and mining operations. The language of LHP offers a primary example. It was presented as aiming for "the greatest social happiness and political stability for the Venezuelan people, under the socialist thinking and action of the Supreme Commander and Leader of the Bolivarian Revolution, Hugo Chávez . . . to continue advancing in the full satisfaction of the basic necessities for the life of our people" (Venezuela 2013, p. 2, 4). The text introducing the LHP to the national legislature made clear Maduro's intentions as he presented the plan for adoption. Maduro, the text informs its readers, stated to the National Elections Council that "I come here today, with the people of Bolívar and Chávez to defend the achievements conquered in 14 years of the Bolivarian Revolution and to ratify . . . the Homeland Plan 2013–2019" (Venezuela 2013,

p. 5). It was the people, in other words, who were putting the plan forward. Indeed, the text reminded readers that when Chávez presented his proposal for the plan to the country, he announced that it would be subject to a "great debate at the grassroots level of the people" for, Chávez continued, it is the people that "will give it depth, legitimacy, and indestructible strength" (ibid.).

Specific extractivist objectives of the LHP were accordingly tied closely to the people and their fate. Objective 1.3.1, for example, stated that the country should "maintain and strengthen the current oil tax regime to guarantee the well-being of the people." Oil revenues would be put to the service of the people. Objective 1.3.8 called on officials to "design and establish innovative and effective mechanisms, aimed at promoting popular participation in oil revenue, such as investment and savings." This meant that average Venezuelans could have direct access to the country's wealth by way of fractional ownership. Along the same lines, Objective 1.3.8.2 sought to "promote the Popular Savings Fund, as a savings mechanism and participation in the oil industry." On the international front, LHP called for better international energy agreements with other countries in Latin America (these were key for Venezuela's ability to sell its oil abroad and earn much needed revenues), again with the general welfare of the Venezuelan people in mind. Objective 1.3.6.1 stated in this regard the need to "strengthen and expand Energy Cooperation Agreements (CCE) to drive the establishment of fair, supportive, efficient and intermediation-free exchange relations in the fight against poverty, reducing economic and social asymmetries" (Venezuela 2013, p. 8).

Maduro would echo such populism at various junctures after Chavez's death. At one point, for instance, he called for grassroots actions by oil workers to take control of oil installations. The struggle against the elites had to rely on the people. In a second instance, after extending the total control of PDVSA to an appointed commission in 2020, in the midst of the COVID-19 pandemic he directed the oil minister (Tareck El Aissami) and the president of PDVSA (Asdrúbal Chávez) to "speak with the working class, to recover everything . . . and to guarantee that our PDVSA shines and flies high for the benefit of our Venezuela." As he spoke, he then reminded those present that "when we speak of oil policy, of the Bolivarian Revolution, we must speak of Comandante Hugo Chávez and of the circumstances that we must face in this period: the total oil sanctions by the North American empire; of the total imperialist persecution of all oil operations in the world that have to do with PDVSA." It followed, Maduro pointed out, that in the struggle against these forces not every decision can be revealed. "It is like a war," he observed, and "do you announce where your army will advance in a war?" Thus, he added, "I ask God, I ask the working class that they make it possible for the miracle of recovery and expansion of the Venezuelan oil industry" (Albaciudad.org 2020). Again, the anti-imperialist struggle against foreign elites had to rely on average Venezuelans – above all those belonging to the working class.

Consistent with this, Maduro also claimed that the development of the Orinoco Mining Arc was, similarly, for the benefit of the Venezuelan people such as small-scale miners and indigenous communities (Rosales 2017, p. 132–133). In his Twitter post promoting the *2019–2025 Mining Sector Plan*, Maduro (NicolasMaduro 2019) declared also that "Venezuela has a Mining Sector Plan 2019–2025 . . . we will move towards the prosperity and happiness of the people."

All this meant that Chávez and Maduro also tied their plans for an extractivist economy by linking it closely to the idea of national sovereignty, which itself was closely tied to a sense of popular self-determination. Referring, for instance, to the need to "defend, expand, and consolidate the most precious good that we have reclaimed after 200 years – national independence," LHP asserted the need to "preserve sovereignty over our oil resources in particular, and natural resources in general" (Venezuela 2013, p. 4). The regime's takeover of the nation's productive assets, in other words, should have been understood as a fundamental step in the struggle to free Venezuela from international and national neocolonial and capitalist interests and its efforts to return power to the people through the plans and actions of a genuinely autonomous state. Observers called the approach "neo-extractivism" (Chiasson-LeBel 2016), to differentiate it from previous forms of extractivism that served elite classes.

8 Reflections on the Populist Approach to the Environment

Present and Futures

The four case studies, drawn from Europe and the Americas, illustrated how populist parties manifest considerable variation in their environmental stances. Their placements in the traditional left to right political spectrum cannot predict those stances. Populists can present positive or negative environmental stances across that spectrum. This is because, as argued in the introduction, populism is largely devoid of *a priori* stances on substantive issues. Its trademark is instead a basic worldview that divides societies into the two groups of 'the pure people' and 'the morally corrupt elites.' Substantive positions of various kinds can be molded in service of that worldview. Those positions become accordingly second-order issues.

The empirical analysis also showed that, despite the observable variations in stances, the four populist parties nonetheless anchored their environmental stances in their rhetoric of people-centrism and anti-elitism. Those stances became conduits for the expression of their populism. In this regard, the parties were similar and, as with their variance in terms of being either pro- or anti-environment, operated in line with the logic of populism. This is what it means to be a populist: to leverage substantive issues in ways that advance the bifurcated view of society as split between a 'pure people' that is suffering at the hands of a 'corrupt elite.' Of course, with this said, we observed that each party articulated their environmental positions in ways consonant with their ideological tendencies (at work since populism, by virtue of being ideologically 'thin,' requires an ideological home), supporters' base, and the political and economic contexts in which they operated. This is what ultimately shaped the specifics of their positions, including the particular dimensions of the environment they focused on – such as resource extraction or small-scale sustainable agriculture.

These findings prompt us to reflect further on the relationship between populism and the environment. As noted from the outset, the objective of this book is to put forth a deductive framework about that relationship derived from the logic of populism itself – in contrast to the existing literature, which has investigated that relationship by considering case studies and then generating inductive conclusions. If the case studies offer convincing evidence in

DOI: 10.4324/9781003423133-9

support of the framework, a number of observations are in order. Two seem especially pressing.

First, it seems fair to assume that the environmental positions of populist parties may be more or less genuine. Since those positions are instrumental to their populist agenda, they do not necessarily reflect deeply held convictions. They are of second-order importance: they are relevant in so far as they help populists promote their identities and what they wish to achieve. As French Green Member of the European Parliament Yannick Jadot argued, for instance, when discussing RN's environmental agenda, "the extreme right say [sic] it was better before because we were all white and Christian – Catholic – and gay weddings were not an issue and we were somehow in a better relation with nature. This is now part of a fake image that they are trying to sell about the former order in terms of family, nature and race" (Neslen 2014). To be clear, the point here is not that all populists must inevitably hold environmental positions in which they do not believe or believe with limited conviction. Rather, it is that environmental stances are not axiomatic principles that define populists: as a result, they may be held with more or less commitment.

The question applies to populists who are positively or negatively inclined toward the environment. Yet, it may be most relevant in the case of the former. Scholars and others have noted that any political party wishing to win at the national level must take a position on the environment (Guillou 2022). Most voters are cognizant of, and worry about, the environmental crisis facing the globe. The consequence of this is that no party can afford to ignore the issue, and in most cases it will be necessary for any one party to express at least some degree of concern. We note here that RN's *New Ecology* was launched at the same time as right-wing populists in Switzerland, Hungary, and Denmark were putting forward their own claims about the need to protect the environment. As Jadot observed on this point, "clearly, there is a trend. Five years ago most of the European extreme right parties were very different, but now they want to have power and be in governments so they have to widen their voting base" (Neslen 2014). Opportunism may be a driver of populists' environmentalism.

Second, it follows that it should not be surprising to see any one party change its positions over time or even maintain inconsistent stances at any given time. Expediency or other considerations may call for shifts in position. After all, the lack of core ideological attachments renders populism malleable, capable of "adjust[ing] to [the] perceptions and needs of different societies" (Mudde and Kaltwasser 2013, p. 150) and times. We can expect the environmentalism of populists, in other words, to show considerable inconsistencies – though, importantly, we should also expect deviating positions to still be anchored in the particular people-centrism and anti-elitism of the populist parties in question. For supporters of populist parties and leaders, this will in turn not be particularly concerning, since their interest in those political actors is primarily due to their populist views and not necessarily their specific substantive positions. At the very least, it seems appropriate to assume that those supporters will exhibit a fair amount of tolerance toward those shifts (an assumption that can apply more generally to shifts in position on any given substantive issue). Moreover, as noted from the outset, the environment is not a monolithic policy area, and various strands of concern can lend themselves to different 'uses' and positionings, in line with the overall orientations of the populist party in question. This might make those positions actually more genuine than might otherwise be presupposed. Initial consideration of some of the case studies examined in this book points to supporting empirical evidence.

When it comes to RN, for instance, its pro-environmental positions represented a turnaround from previous stances – especially those held until 2011, when RN was under the leadership of Le Pen's father, Jean-Marie Le Pen. In fact, well into the 2010s, Marine Le Pen would have been considered a skeptic on climate change. As her popularity and odds of winning the presidential elections increased in the early 2020s, the need to take on more clearly pro-environmental stances became more obvious (Damiani and Pollet 2021). We note, in addition, that Juvin, the architect of RNs' 'nationalistic green localism,' was according to observers the only RN specialist on environmental matters. With environmental protection becoming the second most important issue for French voters in the early 2020s, RN had no choice but to take an explicit and positive stance toward it (Guillou 2022). As it did so, and as we saw in Chapter 4, it, of course, grounded those stances squarely in its populist worldview while selecting environmental themes that conceptually 'fitted' its nationalistic and protectionist principles.

Similarly, Trump's negative stances were occasionally countered by more pro-environmental claims. These, too, were grounded in his populist rhetoric – further confirming that populism, and not the specific substantive positions, are what matters – and were selectively focused on aspects of conservation that, given Trump's ideological tendencies and supporters' base, could lend themselves to positive positions. The bipartisan *Land Conversation Bill* was for instance framed as a "truly landmark legislation that will preserve America's majestic natural wonders, priceless historic treasures . . . these exquisite resources the most glorious heritage a people have ever received" (The Associated Press 2020). Trump's annual *Earth Day* statements included passages such as "America is blessed with some of the most beautiful scenery on Earth. As Americans, we all share an immense pride in these God-given treasures and a tremendous appreciation for our abundance of natural resources . . . we reaffirm our commitment to protecting our natural treasures for the benefit and enjoyment of all Americans" (Trump 2019c). And in his annual *Ocean Awareness Month* remarks, Trump (2020c) highlighted that "our ocean and coastal waterways are essential to our national security . . . global competitiveness, and transportation . . . to promote economic prosperity, create jobs, and strengthen our maritime and homeland security for current and future generations of Americans." We can add here that these were in any case fairly uncontroversial assertions and policies that enjoyed broad bipartisan support and popular approval. As such, to return to the opportunistic point made earlier, they offered easy ways for Trump to appear sensitive to growing concerns about the environment.

We note inconsistencies in Chávez's case too. His speech at the 2009 *UN Climate Change Conferences* in Copenhagen became representative in this regard. He recognized that "climate change is undoubtedly the most devastating environmental problem of this century." He then continued: "Floods, droughts, severe storms, hurricanes, melting ice caps, rise in mean sea levels, ocean acidification and heat waves, all of that sharpens the impact of the global crisis besetting us" (Chávez 2013). Such language represented a remarkable departure from his statements and policies on resource extraction and the use of nonrenewable energy sources. In the same vein, we note that the LHP itself, despite its obvious anti-environmental policies, also contained references to the climate crisis. We stress here again that we need not dismiss wholesale these alternative positions as necessarily not genuine. The point, rather, is to note the divergences and recognize that on the whole they are subservient to the logic of populism and therefore rooted in it, rather than exist as commitment taken as first-order principles.

Hence, as with Trump, Chávez's deviations were consistently anchored in his populist outlook. As his anti-environmental stances, his more positive statements were instruments to project his views on the corrupt capitalist elites of the world and the harms suffered by everyday people who were victims of the neoliberal order. Consistent with that, in the Copenhagen speech, Chávez (ibid.) immediately turned to highlighting what really deserved attention. The fault for the climate crisis, he claimed, was not that of developing countries but capitalists: "Let's talk about the cause, let's not evade responsibilities, and let's not evade the depth of this problem. The cause, undoubtedly . . . is the destructive metabolic system of capital and its embodied model: Capitalism." And here the rich countries were above all guilty: "we are profoundly unequal. . . . Seven percent is responsible, these 500 million richest people are responsible for 50 percent of emissions, while the poorest 50 percent accounts for only seven percent of emissions." Indeed, he added, "if the climate were a bank, it would have been saved already."

Accordingly, Chávez continued, "what we are experiencing on this planet is an imperial dictatorship, and from here we continue denouncing it. . . . There is a group of countries that consider themselves superior to us in the South, to us in the Third World, to us, the underdeveloped countries." Hence Chávez concluded that "we the peoples of the world ask of the empires, to those who try to continue dominating the world and exploiting us . . . let's stop environmental degradation and avoid the great catastrophe of climate change." It followed that the solution would have to come from the people and from socialism. As he put it at one point,

> I have been reading some of the slogans painted on the streets, and I think those slogans of these youngsters, some of which I heard when I was young, and of the young woman there, two of which I noted. You can hear, among others, two powerful slogans. One: Don't change the climate, change the system. And I take it as instructions for us. Let's not change the climate, let's change the system! And consequently we will begin to save the planet. Capitalism is a destructive development model that is putting an end to life; it threatens to put a definitive end to the human species. (ibid.)

Such possibilities of turnarounds and internal inconsistencies raise not only questions about the extent to which populists believe any one position but also the degree to which they could in practice pursue any one of their stances. Goals that stand in opposition to each other cannot be met. It might be useful to ask whether there is a hierarchy among those goals and, with that, perhaps more or less genuine commitment associated with any given goal.

We should also reflect on whether the observable inconsistencies may, at least in the eyes of those who articulate them, be somehow defensible – at least partly because they deal with different dimensions of the environmental crisis. For instance, as we saw Trump's pro-environmental stances were often made in reference to national parks or the natural beauty of the country which, because intricately linked to the character of the nation and its people, deserve protection. Opening remote natural habitats to oil drilling may go against the spirit of those comments, but this involves different parts of the landscape and territory – at least following his logic. Moreover, given that he presented his energy policies as augmenting the country's power and standing in the world, they share something more fundamental with his more protectionist claims: both are about the greatness of the US.

A similar point could be made about Chávez's inconsistencies: a socialist model of production, even if reliant on extractivism, would be more mindful of the environment (while of course also ensuring a broader distribution of wealth to the benefit of everyone) than a capitalist and more destructive model. Chávez could reasonably advance protectionist ideas while pursuing a socialist vision of development that included harmful practices since the vision was set in comparison to what he thought were the more destructive forces of capitalism. Moreover, given Venezuela's heavy economic reliance on natural resource extraction, it could be argued that it would have been impossible for Chávez and Maduro not to pursue extractivist policies – and thus not to adopt correspondingly anti-environmental stances that must necessarily accompany at least in part such policies. This does not mean that the two leaders could also not harbor pro-environmentalist stances and that, when given the opportunity to express those before the world and in the context of a long history of colonialism and neocolonialism, they would seize those openings to offer alternative perspectives.

The findings and these reflections accordingly point to important venues for future research. Concerning the veracity of stances and how they may change over time, it would be fruitful to identify and explain the observable patterns. For this, more cases of populists changing stances – such as Austria's Freedom Party *(Freiheitliche Partei Österreichs)* or Germany's Alternative for Germany *(Alternative für Deutschland)* – would offer additional data. Can the commitments to pro-environmental stances be somehow measured in a reliable and systematic fashion? Are there differences in those commitments between the party leaders and the supporters? As to changes over time, how do populists themselves make sense of their departures from previous positions? How do their supporters view those changes?

The findings also encourage us to reflect on the question of policy impact. Throughout our analysis, our primary focus has been on stances. But knowing more about those stances has potential policy implications, especially for populists in power (Dieckhoff et al. 2022): second-order, potentially inconsistent, and at times vague positions toward the environment are unlikely to generate enough support and resources for sustained action. If we consider that populist parties are often in coalitions with other parties, they may be prone to ceding ground to their partners if deemed useful. This reasoning seems consistent with research that reports negative policy outcomes from populists in leadership positions (Böhmelt 2021). At the same time, the possibility that parties can at times do more on second-order issues than on first-order ones should be kept in mind: facing less scrutiny and pressure, they may be able to 'get away' with initiatives that would otherwise raise questions if these were part of their core platforms.

On a more general level, the four case studies examined in this book are obviously a small subset of all populist parties in the world. Data on more cases would allow for refinement to the proposed framework. It would, for instance, be useful to identify 'families' of populist parties with similar environmental orientations and related populist anchors. This could lead to more analytical sophistication around those anchors – their subtypes for example, or possible variations. For instance, the anti-elitism anchor might exhibit distinct patterns. Hence, we may find that some parties tend to target primarily domestic elites (Podemos offers an example) while others have more of an international outlook (as with Trump, Chávez, and Maduro). In turn, perhaps right-leaning populist parties are more likely to anchor their environmentalism in some form of 'exclusive' nationalism (Dunn 2013), calling for the protection of national territories from foreign interference. Left-leaning ones, by contrast, may be more inclined to seek solutions internationally (as, for instance, with Venezuela and its participation in UN initiatives).

References

Agence France Presse. (2002, Dec 19). *Venezuela's Chavez Says Revolution Must 'Clean Up' PDVSA*. https://www.afp.com/en

Agnew, J., and Shin, M. (2017). Spatializing Populism: Taking Politics to the People in Italy. *Annals of the American Association of Geographers 107*(4), 915–933. https://doi.org/10.1080/24694452.2016.1270194

Aisch, G., Bloch, M., Lai, K. K. R., and Morenne, B. (2017, May 7). How France Voted. *The New York Times*. www.nytimes.com/interactive/2017/05/07/world/europe/france-election-results-maps.html

Akkerman, T. (2012). Immigration Policy and Electoral Competition in Western Europe: A Fine-Grained Analysis of Party Positions Over the Past Two Decades. *Party Politics 21*(1), 54–67. https://doi.org/10.1177/1354068812462928

Albaciudad.org (2020, Aug 20). *Presidente Maduro Prorroga la 'Comisión Presidencial Alí Rodriguez Araque' en Pdvsa*. www.aporrea.org/energia/n358105.html

Albertazzi, D., and McDonnell, D. (2008). Introduction: The Sceptre and the Spectre. In D. Albertazzi and D. McDonnell (Eds.), *Twenty-First Century Populism: The Spectre of Western European Democracy* (p. 1–11). Palgrave Macmillan. https://doi.org/10.1057/9780230592100_1

Anapol, A. (2017, Oct 19). Trump's Pick for Environmental Job Once Called Belief in Global Warming 'Paganism.' *The Hill*. https://thehill.com/homenews/administration/356281-trumps-pick-for-environmental-official-once-called-belief-in-global/

Andreucci, D. (2018). Populism, Hegemony, and the Politics of Natural Resource Extraction in Evo Morales's Bolivia. *Antipode 50*(4), 825–845. https://doi.org/10.1111/anti.12373

Assemblée Nationale. (2014, Oct 1) *Amendment N. 2285*. www.assemblee-nationale.fr/14/amendements/2230/AN/2285.asp

The Associated Press. (2020). Trump Stumbles Over the Word 'Yosemite' During Bill Signing [Video]. *The New York Times*. www.nytimes.com/video/us/100000007272140/trump-stumbles-over-yosemite.html

Babson, S. (2023). *Forgotten Populists: When Farmers Turned Left to Save Democracy*. Mission Point Press.

Baena, C. E. (2019). *The Policy Process in a Petro-State: An Analysis of PDVSA's (Petróleos de Venezuela SA's) Internationalisation Strategy*. Routledge.

68   *References*

Baléo, M. (2020, June 26). Hervé Juvin, L'Artisan de la Nouvelle Doctrine du Rassemblement National. *Le Grand Continent*. https://legrandcontinent.eu/fr/2020/06/26/herve-juvin-lartisan-de-la-nouvelle-doctrine-du-rassemblement-national/

Balthazar, A. C. (2017). Made in Britain: Brexit, Teacups, and the Materiality of the Nation. *American Ethnologist 44*(2), 220–224. https://doi.org/10.1111/amet.12471

Batel, S., and Devine-Wright, P. (2018). Populism, Identities and Responses to Energy Infrastructures at Different Scales in the United Kingdom: A Post-Brexit Reflection. *Energy Research & Social Science 43*, 41–47. https://doi.org/10.1016/j.erss.2018.05.011

Bauduin, C. (2017, Mar 8). Marine Le Pen sur RTL: La Taxation du Diesel, 'un Scandale à l'Égard des Classes Modestes.' *RTL*. www.rtl.fr/actu/politique/marine-le-pen-sur-rtl-la-taxation-du-diesel-un-scandale-a-l-egard-des-classes-modestes-7787572760

Berg, R. C. (2021, Oct 12). The Role of the Oil Sector in Venezuela's Environmental Degradation and Economic Rebuilding. *Center for Strategic and National Studies*. www.csis.org/analysis/role-oil-sector-venezuelas-environmental-degradation-and-economic-rebuilding

Böhmelt, T. (2021). Populism and Environmental Performance. *Global Environmental Politics 21*(3), 97–123. https://doi.org/10.1162/glep_a_00606

Bonikowski, B. (2016). Three Lessons of Contemporary Populism in Europe and the United States. *The Brown Journal of World Affairs 23*(1), 9–24. www.jstor.org/stable/26534707

Brubaker, R. (2017). Why Populism? *Theory and Society 46*(5), 357–385. https://doi.org/10.1007/s11186-017-9301-7

Buxton, J. (2003). Economic Policy and the Rise of Hugo Chávez. In S. Ellner and D. Hellinger (Eds.), *Venezuelan Politics in the Chávez Era: Class, Polarization & Conflict* (p. 113–130). Lynne Rienner Publishers.

Buzogány, A., and Mohamad-Klotzbach, C. (2021). Populism and Nature – the Nature of Populism: New Perspectives on the Relationship Between Populism, Climate Change, and Nature Protection. *Zeitschrift für Vergleichende Politikwissenschaft 15*(2), 155–164. https://doi.org/10.1007/s12286-021-00492-7

Buzogány, A., and Mohamad-Klotzbach, C. (2022). Environmental Populism. In M. Oswald (Eds.), *The Palgrave Handbook of Populism* (p. 321–340). Springer International Publishing.

Caiani, M., and Lubarda, B. (2023). Conditional Environmentalism of Right-Wing Populism in Power: Ideology and/or Opportunities? *Environmental Politics*. https://doi.org/10.1080/09644016.2023.2242749

Campbell, J. L. (2018). *American Discontent: The Rise of Donald Trump and Decline of the Golden Age*. Oxford University Press.

Campbell, J. L. (2023). *Institutions Under Siege: Donald Trump's Attack on the Deep State*. Cambridge University Press.

Canovan, M. (1999). Trust the People! Populism and the Two Faces of Democracy. *Political Studies 47*(1), 2–16. https://doi.org/10.1111/1467-9248.00184

Carlson, A. (2017). Climate Change, Trump and Populism [Conference Paper]. *The Future of the Global Order Colloquium*. https://global.upenn. edu/sites/default/files/go-climate-change-carlson.original.pdf

Ćetković, S., and Hagemann, C. (2020). Changing Climate for Populists? Examining the Influence of Radical-Right Political Parties on Low-Carbon Energy Transitions in Western Europe. *Energy Research & Social Science* 66, Article 101571. https://doi.org/10.1016/j.erss.2020.101571

Chávez, H. (2013, May 6). Hugo Chávez on Climate Change and Capitalism. *Climate & Capitalism*. https://climateandcapitalism.com/2013/03/06/hugo-chavez-on-climate-change-and-capitalism/

Chiasson-LeBel, T. (2016). Neo-Extractivism in Venezuela and Ecuador: A Weapon of Class Conflict. *The Extractive Industries and Society 3*(4), 888–901. https://doi.org/10.1016/j.exis.2016.10.006

Collectif Nouvelle Ecologie. (2015, Oct 26). Pollution par les Diesel Volkswagen: La Commission Européenne Savait, Elle a Menti. *Rassemblement National*. https://rassemblementnational.fr/communiques/pollution-par-les-diesel-volkswagen-la-commission-europeenne-savait-elle-a-menti/

Collectif Nouvelle Ecologie. (2016, Oct 17). Accords de Kigali: Oui à des Accords Internationaux de Bon Sens. *Rassemblement National*. https://rassemblementnational.fr/communiques/accords-de-kigali-oui-a-des-accords-internationaux-de-bon-sens

Collectif Nouvelle Ecologie. (2017, Jul 27). Les États Généraux de l'Alimentation Aborderont-ils les Vrais Problèmes? *Rassemblement National*. https://rassemblementnational.fr/communiques/les-etats-generaux-de-lalimentation-aborderont-ils-les-vrais-problemes/

Curato, N. (2017). Flirting with Authoritarian Fantasies? Rodrigo Duterte and the New Terms of Philippine Populism. *Journal of Contemporary Asia* 47(1), 142–153. https://doi.org/10.1080/00472336.2016.1239751

Damiani, A., and Pollet, M. (2021, Apr 7). Bye Frexit, Hello Ecology: Why Le Pen's Party Programme Has a New Agenda. *Euractiv*. www.euractiv.com/section/elections/news/bye-frexit-hello-ecology-why-le-pens-party-programme-has-a-new-agenda/

Davenport, C. (2020, Aug 10). EPA to Lift Obama-Era Controls on Methane, a Potent Greenhouse Gas. *The New York Times*. www.nytimes.com/2020/08/10/climate/trump-methane-climate-change.html

de la Torre, C. (2018). Populism Revived: Donald Trump and the Latin American Leftist Populists. *The Americas 75*(4), 733–753. https://doi.org/10.1017/tam.2018.39

de la Torre, C. (2019). *Routledge Handbook of Global Populism*. Routledge.

de Nadal, L. (2021, Aug 23). Spain's VOX Party and the Rise of International Environmental Populism. *Green European Journal*. www.greeneuropeanjournal.eu/spains-vox-party-and-the-rise-of-international-environmental-populism/

de Saint-Just, W. (2015, May 18). Pollution de l'Air: M. Najdovski Veut Enfumer la Banlieue. *Rassemblement National*. https://rassemblementnational.fr/communiques/pollution-de-lair-m-najdovski-veut-enfumer-la-banlieue/

Dieckhoff, A., Jaffrelot, C., and Massicard, É. (2022). *Contemporary Populists in Power*. Springer International Publishing.

Doyle, A., and Farand, C. (2020, Jan 21). Trump Criticises 'Prophets of Doom' in Davos and Touts Fossil Fuels. *Climate Home News*. www.climat-echangenews.com/2020/01/21/trump-criticises-prophets-doom-davos-touts-fossil-fuels/

Duina, F., and Carson, D. (2019). Not So Right After All? Making Sense of the Progressive Rhetoric of Europe's Far-Right Parties. *International Sociology 35*(1), 3–21. https://doi.org/10.1177/0268580919881862

Dunn, K. (2013). Preference for Radical Right-Wing Populist Parties among Exclusive-Nationalists and Authoritarians. *Party Politics 21*(3), 367–380. https://doi.org/10.1177/1354068812472587

Durand, M. (2021, March 9). Ecologie: Marine Le Pen Présente Son Contre-Project de Référendum. *Le Journal du Dimanche*. lejdd.fr. https://www.lejdd.fr/Politique/ecologie-marine-le-pen-presente-son-contre-projet-de-referendum-4030232

Ebus, B. (2018, Aug 9). Venezuela's Mining Crisis Gains Regional Attention. *Earth Island Journal*. www.earthisland.org/journal/index.php/articles/entry/venezuelas-mining-crisis-gains-regional-attention/

Errejón, I. (2014, July 15). Spain's Podemos: An Inside View of a Radical Left Sensation. *LINKS: International Journal of Socialist Renewal*. http://links.org.au/node/3969

European Commission. (2007). *Venezuela Country Strategy Paper 2007–2013 (E/2007/622)*. https://eeas.europa.eu/archives/docs/venezuela/csp/07_13_en.pdf

Farley, J. E. (2019). Five Decisive States: Examining How and Why Donald Trump Won the 2016 Election. *Sociological Quarterly 60*(3), 337–353. https://doi.org/10.1080/00380253.2019.1629847

Farnsworth, E. (2021, Feb 22). Deconstructing Chavismo: The Myth and the Reality. *American Society Council of the Americas*. www.as-coa.org/articles/deconstructing-chavismo-myth-and-reality

Fominaya, C. F. (2014, Jun 4). 'Spain is Different:' Podemos and 15-M. *London School of Economics and Political Science*. https://blogs.lse.ac.uk/eurocrisispress/2014/06/04/spain-is-different-podemos-and-15-m/

Forchtner, B. (2019). Climate Change and the Far Right. *WIREs Climate Change 10*(5), Article e604. https://doi.org/10.1002/wcc.604

Fountain, H., and Eder, S. (2018, Dec 3). In the Blink of an Eye, a Hunt for Oil Threatens Pristine Alaska. *The New York Times*. www.nytimes.com/2018/12/03/us/oil-drilling-arctic-national-wildlife-refuge.html

François, S., and Adrien, N. (2021, Feb 1). 'Identitarian Ecology' the Far Right's Reinterpretation of Environmental Concerns. *Illiberalism Studies Program*. www.illiberalism.org/identitarian-ecology-rights-reinterpretation-environmental-concerns/

Friedman, L. (2019a, Oct 23). Trump Administration to Begin Official Withdrawal from Paris Climate Accord. *The New York Times*. www.nytimes.com/2019/10/23/climate/trump-paris-climate-accord.html?searchResultPosition=1

Friedman, L. (2019b, June 19). EPA Finalizes Its Plan to Replace Obama-Era Climate Rules. *The New York Times*. www.nytimes.com/2019/06/19/climate/epa-coal-emissions.html

Friedman, L. (2021, Oct 6). Trump Weakens Environmental Law to Expedite Construction Permits. *The New York Times*. www.nytimes.com/2020/07/15/climate/trump-environment-nepa.html?searchResultPosition=1

Friedman, L., and Davenport, C. (2019, Sep 12). Trump Administration Rolls Back Clean Water Protections. *The New York Times*. www.nytimes.com/2019/09/12/climate/trump-administration-rolls-back-clean-water-protections.html?searchResultPosition=3

Front National. (2015, Nov 30). Libre-Échange et Mondialisation Forcée, les Vraies Menaces pour l' Environnement et la Planète. *Rassemblement National*. https://rassemblementnational.fr/communiques/libre-echange-et-mondialisation-forcee-les-vraies-menaces-pour-lenvironnement-et-la-planete/

Gallego, B. A. (2019, Oct 10). Podemos se Desmarca del Green New Deal Para Abordar el 'Origen' de la Crisis Climática. *Público*. www.publico.es/politica/elecciones-10-n-separa-green-new-deal-abordar-origen-crisis-climatica-cree-green-new-deal-no-suficiente-enfrentar-crisis-climatica.html?utm_source=twitter&utm_medium=social&utm_campaign=web

Gallie, W. B. (2019). Essentially Contested Concepts. In B. Max (Ed.), *The Importance of Language* (p. 121–146). Cornell University Press. https://doi.org/10.7591/9781501741319-010

Gilmartin, E., and Greene, T. (2019, Apr 28). Podemos's Green New Deal: An Interview with Txema Guijarro. *Jacobin*. https://jacobin.com/2019/04/podemos-green-new-deal-pablo-iglesias

Gonzales, R., Siegler, K., and Dwyer, C. (2017, Dec 14). Trump Orders Largest National Monument Reduction in US History. *NPR*. www.npr.org/sections/thetwo-way/2017/12/04/567803476/trump-dramatically-shrinks-2-utah-national-monuments

Goodliffe, G. (2015). Europe's Salience and 'Owning' Euroscepticism: Explaining the Front National's Victory in the 2014 European Elections in France. *French Politics 13*(4), 324–345. https://doi.org/10.1057/fp.2015.19

Gross, S. (2020, Aug 4). What Is the Trump Administration's Track Record on the Environment? *Brookings*. www.brookings.edu/articles/what-is-the-trump-administrations-track-record-on-the-environment/

Guillou, C. (Dec 9, 2022). France's Far-Right Rassemblement National Looks to Redefine Environmental Policy. *Le Monde*. www.lemonde.fr/en/politics/article/2022/12/09/france-s-far-right-rassemblement-national-looks-to-redefine-environmental-policy_6007169_5.html

Hancox, D. (2015, Feb 2). Why Ernesto Laclau Is the Intellectual Figurehead for Syriza and Podemos. *The Guardian*. www.theguardian.com/commentisfree/2015/feb/09/ernesto-laclau-intellectual-figurehead-syriza-podemos

Hawkins, K. A. (2009). Is Chávez Populist? Measuring Populist Discourse in Comparative Perspective. *Comparative Political Studies 42*(8), 1040–1067. https://doi.org/10.1177/0010414009331721

Heinisch, R., Holtz-Bacha, C., and Mazzoleni, O. (2021). *Political Populism: Handbook of Concepts, Questions and Strategies of Research*. Nomos Verlag.

Heinrich Boell Foundation. (2012). *The Orinoco Oil Belt – Update*. www.boell.de/sites/default/files/uploads/2012/10/venezuela-orinoco.pdf

Hellinger, D. (2016). Oil and the Chávez Legacy. *Latin American Perspectives 44*(1), 54–77. https://doi.org/10.1177/0094582X16651236

Hellinger, D. (2021, Feb 5). Maduro's Brown New Deal for Venezuela. *North American Congress on Latin America.* https://nacla.org/venezuela-pvd-oil-maduro

Henley, J. (2023, Sep 21). Revealed: One in Three Europeans Now Vote Anti-Establishment. *The Guardian.* www.theguardian.com/world/2023/sep/21/revealed-one-in-three-europeans-now-votes-anti-establishment? CMP=Share_AndroidApp_Other

Huber, R. A., Greussing, E., and Eberl, J-M. (2021). From Populism to Climate Scepticism: The Role of Institutional Trust and Attitudes towards Science. *Environmental Politics 31*(7), 1115–1138. https://doi.org/10.1080/09644016.2021.1978200

Inglehart, R. F., and Norris, P. (2016). Trump, Brexit, and the Rise of Populism: Economic Have-Nots and Cultural Backlash. *HKS Working Paper No. RWP16–026.* http://doi.org/10.2139/ssrn.2818659

Irfan, U. (2019, Jun 19). Trump's EPA Just Replaced Obama's Signature Climate Policy with a Much Weaker Rule. *Vox.* www.vox.com/2019/6/19/18684054/climate-change-clean-power-plan-repeal-affordable-emissions

Jahn, D. (2021). Quick and Dirty: How Populist Parties in Government Affect Greenhouse Gas Emissions in EU Member States. *Journal of European Public Policy 28*(7), 980–997. https://doi.org/10.1080/13501763.2021.1918215

Jansen, R. S. (2011). Populist Mobilization: A New Theoretical Approach to Populism. *Sociological Theory 29*(2), 75–96. https://doi.org/10.1111/j.1467-9558.2011.01388.x

Juvin, H. (2019, Dec 16). 'Green Deal,' Réalités et Illusions Écologiques. *Site Officiel d'Hervé Juvin.* https://hervejuvin.com/green-deal-ecologie-humaine/

Kaltwasser, C. R., Taggart, P. A., Espejo, P. O., and Ostiguy, P. (2017). *The Oxford Handbook of Populism.* Oxford University Press.

Kassam, A. (2014, May 27). Podemos Hopes to Cement Rise of Citizen Politics in Spain after Election Success. *The Guardian.* www.theguardian.com/politics/2014/may/27/podemos-citizen-politics-spain-elections-indignados-movement

Kaya, A. (2021). The Use of the Past by the Alternative for Germany and the Front National: Heritage Populism, Ostalgia and Jeanne D'Arc. *Journal of Contemporary European Studies 31*(2), 318–331. https://doi.org/10.1080/14782804.2021.1981835

Kenny, M. (2017). Back to the Populist Future? Understanding Nostalgia in Contemporary Ideological Discourse. *Journal of Political Ideologies 22*(3), 256–273. https://doi.org/10.17863/CAM.11108

Kojola, E. (2019). Bringing Back the Mines and a Way of Life: Populism and the Politics of Extraction. *Annals of the American Association of Geographers 109*(2), 371–381. https://doi.org/10.1080/24694452.2018.1506695

Köllner, P., Sil, R., and Ahram, A. I. (2018). Comparative Area Studies: What It Is, What It Can Do. In A. I. Ahram, P. Köllner and R. Sil (Eds.), *Comparative Area Studies: Methodological Rationales and Cross-regional Applications* (p. 3–26). Oxford University Press.

Kramarz, T., and Kingsbury, D. V. (2022). Climate Action and Populism of the Left in Ecuador. *Environmental Politics 31*(5), 841–860. https://doi.org/10. 1080/09644016.2022.2090388

Kulin, J., Sevä, I. J., and Dunlap, R. E. (2021). Nationalist Ideology, Right-wing Populism, and Public Views about Climate Change in Europe. *Environmental Politics 30*(7), 1111–1134. https://doi.org/10.1080/09644016. 2021.1898879

Laclau, E. (2005a). *On Populist Reason*. Verso.

Laclau, E. (2005b). Populism: What's in a Name? In Panizza, F. (Ed.), *Populism and the Mirror of Democracy* (p. 32–49). Verso.

La Tribune. (2019, Feb 18). Le Pen Claims to Be Spokesperson for 'Real Yellow Vests.' *Euractiv*. www.euractiv.com/section/eu-elections-2019/news/le-pen-claims-to-be-spokesperson-for-real-yellow-vests/

Le Pen, M. (2017a, Mar 7). *144 Engagements Présidentiels*. www.politique-animaux.fr/fichiers/prises-de-positions/pieces-jointes/projet-presidentiel-marine-le-pen-2017.pdf

Le Pen, M. (2017b, Mar 9). Presidential Campaign Launch – March 9, 2017. *Iowa State University Archives of Women's Political Communication*. https://awpc.cattcenter.iastate.edu/2017/09/01/presidential-campaign-launch-march-9-2017/

Le Pen, M. (2017c, Jun 2). Rebondir Après la Décision Américaine. *Rassemblement National*. https://rassemblementnational.fr/communiques/rebondir-apres-la-decision-americaine/

Lewis, P., Barr, C., Clarke, S., Voce, A., Levett, C., and Gutiérrez, P. (2019, Mar 6). Revealed: The Rise and Rise of Populist Rhetoric. *The Guardian*. www.theguardian.com/world/ng-interactive/2019/mar/06/revealed-the-rise-and-rise-of-populist-rhetoric

Lewis, P., Clarke, S., Barr, C., Holder, J., and Kommenda, N. (2019, Nov 20). Revealed: One in Four Europeans Vote Populist. *The Guardian*. www.theguardian.com/world/ng-interactive/2018/nov/20/revealed-one-in-four-europeans-vote-populist

Lherm, T. (2015, Mar 25). Loi Biodiversité: Non à la Bobo-Écologie Punitive! *Politique & Animaux*. www.politique-animaux.fr/chasse/pour-defendre-chasse-les-deputes-du-rbm-ont-vote-contre-le-projet-de-loi-sur-biodiversite

Lockwood, M. (2018). Right-Wing Populism and the Climate Change Agenda: Exploring the Linkages. *Environmental Politics 27*(4), 712–732. https://doi.org/10.1080/09644016.2018.1458411

Lyall, A. M., and Valdivia, G. (2019). The Speculative Petro-State: Volatile Oil Prices and Resource Populism in Ecuador. *Annals of the American Association of Geographers 109*(2), 349–360. https://doi.org/10.1080/24694 452.2018.1531690

Machin, A., and Wagener, O. (2019, Feb 22). The Nature of Green Populism? *Green European Journal*. www.greeneuropeanjournal.eu/the-nature-of-green-populism/

Marquardt, J., Oliveira, M. C., and Lederer, M. (2022). Same, Same But Different? How Democratically Elected Right-Wing Populists Shape Climate Change Policymaking. *Environmental Politics 31*(5), 777–800. https://doi.org/10.1080/09644016.2022.2053423

Martin, A.-C. (2014, Dec 17). Le Pen Launches 'Patriotic' Environmental Movement. *Euractiv*. www.euractiv.com/section/sustainable-dev/news/le-pen-launches-patriotic-environmental-movement/

Mazoue, A. (2019, Apr 20). Le Pen's National Rally Goes Green in Bid for European Election Votes. *France 24*. www.france24.com/en/20190420-le-pen-national-rally-front-environment-european-elections-france

McCarthy, J. (2019). Authoritarianism, Populism, and the Environment: Comparative Experiences, Insights, and Perspectives. *Annals of the American Association of Geographers 109*(2), 301–313. https://doi.org/10.1080/24694452.2018.1554393

Menezes, R. G., and Barbosa Jr., R. (2021). Environmental Governance under Bolsonaro: Dismantling Institutions, Curtailing Participation, Delegitimising Opposition. *Zeitschrift für Vergleichende Politikwissenschaft 15*(2), 229–247. https://doi.org/10.1007/s12286-021-00491-8

Milman, O. (2021, Nov 21). Climate Denial Is Waning on the Right. What's Replacing It Might Be Just as Scary. *The Guardian*. www.theguardian.com/environment/2021/nov/21/climate-denial-far-right-immigration

Moffitt, B. (2016). *The Global Rise of Populism: Performance, Political Style, and Representation*. Stanford University Press.

Moffitt, B., and Tormey, S. (2014). Rethinking Populism: Politics, Mediatisation and Political Style. *Political Studies 62*(2), 381–397. https://doi.org/10.1111/1467-9248.12032

Morel, S. (2023, Jun 23). Lessons from the Debacle of Podemos and the Spanish Radical Left. *Le Monde*. www.lemonde.fr/en/opinion/article/2023/06/23/lessons-from-the-debacle-of-podemos-and-the-spanish-radical-left_6035766_23.html

Mudde, C. (2004). The Populist Zeitgeist. *Government and Opposition 39*(4), 541–563. https://doi.org/10.1111/j.1477-7053.2004.00135.x

Mudde, C. (2013). Three Decades of Populist Radical Right Parties in Western Europe: So What? *European Journal of Political Research 52*(1), 1–19. https://doi.org/10.1111/j.1475-6765.2012.02065.x

Mudde, C. (2017). Populism: An Ideational Approach. In C. R. Kaltwasser, P. Taggart, P. O. Espejo and P. Ostiguy (Eds.), *The Oxford Handbook of Populism* (p. 27–47). Oxford University Press. https://doi.org/10.1093/oxfordhb/9780198803560.013.1

Mudde, C., and Kaltwasser, C. R. (2013). Exclusionary vs. Inclusionary Populism: Comparing Contemporary Europe and Latin America. *Government and Opposition 48*(2), 147–174. https://doi.org/10.1017/gov.2012.11

Mudde, C., and Kaltwasser, C. R. (2017). *Populism: A Very Short Introduction*. Oxford University Press.

Muno, W., and Pfeiffer, C. (2021). *Populismus an der Macht: Strategien und Folgen Populistischen Regierungshandelns*. Springer.

Murer, P., and Richermoz, É. (2015, May 19). Pollution de l' Air dans le Métro, Mettons Fin à l' Enfumage. *Rassemblement National*. https://rassemblementnational.fr/communiques/pollution-de-lair-dans-le-metro-mettons-fin-a-lenfumage/

Murer, P., and Richermoz, É. (2016, Dec 21). Oui à la Prolongation de la Durée de Vie des Centrales Nucléaires de 10 Ans Mais avec un EDF 100% Public.

Rassemblement National. https://rassemblementnational.fr/communiques/seul-le-frexit-nous-protegera-des-perturbateurs-endocriniens/

Myadar, O., and Jackson, S. (2019). Contradictions of Populism and Resource Extraction: Examining the Intersection of Resource Nationalism and Accumulation by Dispossession in Mongolia. *Annals of the American Association of Geographers 109*(2), 361–370. https://doi.org/10.1080/246 94452.2018.1500233

Neslen, A. (2014, Dec 8). French National Front Launches Nationalist Environmental Movement. *The Guardian.* www.theguardian.com/environment/2014/dec/18/french-national-front-launches-nationalist-environmental-movement

NicolasMaduro. (2019, Jun 6). [Twitter]. https://twitter.com/NicolasMaduro/status/1136694180812660736

Norris, P. (2004). Does PR Promote Political Extremism, Redux. *Representation 40*(3), 226–229. https://doi.org/10.1080/00344890408523268

Norris, P., and Inglehart, R. (2019). *Cultural Backlash: Trump, Brexit, and Authoritarian Populism.* Cambridge University Press.

Notilogía. (2016, Feb 24). *Gaceta Oficial N° 40.855 Creación del Arco Minero del Orinoco.* www.notilogia.com/2016/02/gaceta-oficial-n-40-855-creacion-del-arco-minero-del-orinoco.html

Odell, J. S. (2003). Case Study Methods in International Political Economy. *International Studies Perspectives 2*(2), 161–176. https://doi.org/10.1111/1528-3577.00047

Odoul, J. (2018, Mar 14). L'Union Européenne Interdit Enfin les Pesticides Tueurs d' Abeilles Après 30 Ans de Massacre. *Rassemblement National.* https://rassemblementnational.fr/communiques/lunion-europeenne-interdit-enfin-les-pesticides-tueurs-dabeilles-apres-30-ans-de-massacre/

Oliver, J. E., and Rahn, W. M. (2016). Rise of the Trumpenvolk: Populism in the 2016 Election. *The ANNALS of the American Academy of Political and Social Science 667*(1), 189–206. https://doi.org/10.1177/0002716216662639

Onishi, N. (2019, Oct 17). France's Far Right Wants to Be an Environmental Party, Too. *The New York Times.* www.nytimes.com/2019/10/17/world/europe/france-far-right-environment.html?searchResultPosition=9

Orriols, L., and Cordero, G. (2016). The Breakdown of the Spanish Two-Party System: The Upsurge of Podemos and Ciudadanos in the 2015 General Election. *South European Society & Politics 21*(4), 469–492. https://doi.org/10.1080/13608746.2016.1198454

Oswald, M. (2022). *The Palgrave Handbook of Populism.* Springer.

Oswald, M., Fromm, M., and Broda, E. (2021). Strategic Clustering in Right-Wing Populism? 'Green Policies' in Germany and France. *Zeitschrift für Vergleichende Politikwissenschaft 15*(2), 185–205. https://doi.org/10.1007/s12286-021-00485-6

Otteni, C., and Weisskircher, M. (2022). Global Warming and Polarisation: Wind Turbines and the Electoral Success of the Greens and the Populist Radical Right. *European Journal of Political Research 61*(4), 1102–1122. https://doi.org/10.1111/1475-6765.12487

Palmigiani, F. (2021, Jan 19). 'We Are Prepared:' Maduro Pledges to Triple Venezuela Oil Production This Year. *Upstream.* www.upstreamonline.

com/production/we-are-prepared-maduro-pledges-to-triple-venezuela-oil-production-this-year/2-1-947460

Parker, D. (2005). Chávez and the Search for an Alternative to Neoliberalism. *Latin American Perspectives 32*(2), 39–50. www.jstor.org/stable/30040275

Pellegrini, V. (2023). Populist Ideology, Ideological Attitudes, and Anti-Immigration Attitudes as an Integrated System of Beliefs. *PLoS ONE 18*(1), Article e0280285. https://doi.org/10.1371/journal.pone.0280285

Pew Research Center. (2018, Aug 6). *For Most Trump Voters, 'Very Warm' Feelings for Him Endured: An Examination of the 2016 Electorate, Based on Validated Voters.* www.pewresearch.org/politics/2018/08/09/an-examination-of-the-2016-electorate-based-on-validated-voters/

Phillips, T. (2019, Jan 10). Maduro Starts New Venezuela Term by Accusing US of Imperialist 'World War'. *The Guardian.* www.theguardian.com/world/2019/jan/10/venezuela-president-nicolas-maduro-begins-second-term

Podemos. (2015, Jun 5). *Comunicado del Área de Medio Ambiente, Energía y Políticas Urbanas por el Día Mundial del Medio Ambiente.* https://podemos.info/comunicado-del-area-de-medio-ambiente-energia-y-politicas-urbanas-por-el-dia-mundial-del-medio-ambiente/

Podemos. (2016, Nov 24). *Pobreza Energética en España: Situación Actual, Causas y Medidas Para Terminar con Ella.* https://podemos.info/pobreza-energetica-espana-situacion-actual-causas-medidas-terminar/

Podemos. (2018, Mar 19). El Campo no Es una Fábrica. Reforma de la PAC 2020 [Video]. *YouTube.* www.youtube.com/watch?v=nHjm7wtZhyc

Podemos. (2019a, Mar 11). *Podemos Quiere Situar a España en la Vanguardia de la Lucha Contra el Cambio Climático y Propone el 'Plan Horizonte Verde.'* https://podemos.info/podemos-quiere-situar-espana-vanguardia-lucha-contra-cambio-climatico-propone-plan-horizonte-verde/

Podemos. (2019b, Mar 15). Un 'New Deal Verde' Frente al Cambio Climático [Video]. *YouTube.* www.youtube.com/watch?v=FD04O1utvtI

Podemos Environmental Area. (2017, Oct 17). Incendios: Comunicado del Área de Medio Ambiente de Podemos. *Podemos.* https://podemos.info/incendios-comunicado-del-area-medio-ambiente-podemos/

Popovich, N., Albeck-Ripka, L., and Peierre-Louis, K. (2021, Jan 20). The Trump Administration Rolled Back More Than 100 Environmental Rules. Here's the Full List. *The New York Times.* www.nytimes.com/interactive/2020/climate/trump-environment-rollbacks-list.html

Ramalho, T. M. (2023, Aug 8). Podemos and Syrize, the End of an Era? *The Green European Journal.* www.greeneuropeanjournal.eu/podemos-and-syriza-the-end-of-an-era/

Rassemblement National. (2021). *15 Questions sur L'Environnement, Conter-Project de Référendum.* https://reporterre.net/IMG/pdf/le_contre-projet_du_rn_pour_l_ecologie.pdf

realdonaldtrump. (2019, Sept 18). [Twitter]. https://twitter.com/realdonaldtrump/status/1174342164983107584

Rendon, M., Sandin, L., and Fernandez, C. (2020, Apr 16). Illegal Mining in Venezuela: Death and Devastation in the Amazonas and Orinoco Regions. *CSIS Briefs.* www.csis.org/analysis/illegal-mining-venezuela-death-and-devastation-amazonas-and-orinoco-regions

Riedel, R. (2021). Green Conservatism or Environmental Nativism? *Zeitschrift für Vergleichende Politikwissenschaft 15*(2), 207–227. https://doi.org/10.1007/s12286-021-00490-9

Rios, B. (2019, Nov 13). Socialists and Podemos Reach Deal for a 'Progressive' Government in Spain. *Euractiv*. www.euractiv.com/section/elections/news/socialists-and-podemos-reach-deal-for-a-progressive-government-in-spain/

Roberts, K. (2012). Populism and Democracy in Venezuela under Hugo Chávez. In C. Mudde and C. R. Kaltwasser (Eds.), *Populism in Europe and the Americas: Threat or Corrective for Democracy?* (p. 136–159). Cambridge University Press.

Rodríguez-Teruel, J., Barrio, A., and Barberà, O. (2016). Fast and Furious: Podemos' Quest for Power in Multi-level Spain. *South European Society and Politics 21*(4), 561–585. https://doi.org/10.1080/13608746.2016.1250397

Rosales, A. (2017). Venezuela's Deepening Logic of Extraction. *NACLA Report on the Americas 49*(2), 132–135. https://doi.org/10.1080/10714839.2017.1331794

Sagarzazu, I., and Thies, C. G. (2019). The Foreign Policy Rhetoric of Populism: Chávez, Oil, and Anti-imperialism. *Political Research Quarterly 72*(1), 205–214. https://doi.org/10.1177/1065912918784212

Saguin, K. (2019). 'Return the Lake to the People:' Populist Political Rhetoric and the Fate of a Resource Frontier in the Philippines. *Annals of the American Association of Geographers 109*(2), 434–442. https://doi.org/10.1080/24694452.2018.1483815

Salerno, C. (2012, Dec 11). Venezuela's Doha Climate Delegate Talks: 'Rich Countries Profit from Pollution.' *Democracy Now, Venezuelanalysis*. https://venezuelanalysis.com/analysis/7541/

Sandford, A. (2017, Feb 9). What Are Marine Le Pen's Policies? *Euronews*. www.euronews.com/2017/02/09/what-do-we-know-about-marine-le-pens-policies

Schaller, S., and Carius, A. (2019). Convenient Truth: Mapping Climate Agendas of Right-Wing Populist Parties in Europe. *Adelphi Consult GmbH*. www.adelphi.de/en/system/files/mediathek/bilder/Convenient%20Truths%20-%20Mapping%20climate%20agendas%20of%20right-wing%20populist%20parties%20in%20Europe%20-%20adelphi.pdf

Schatzker, E., Laya, P., and Vasquez, A. (2021, Jun 18). Venezuela's Maduro Pleads for Foreign Capital, Biden Deal in Caracas. *BNN Bloomberg*. www.bnnbloomberg.ca/venezuela-s-maduro-pleads-for-foreign-capital-biden-deal-in-caracas-interview-1.1618644

Selk, V., and Kemmerzell, J. (2022). Retrogradism in Context: Varieties of Right-Wing Populist Climate Politics. *Environmental Politics 31*(5), 755–776. https://doi.org/10.1080/09644016.2021.1999150

Sola, J., and Rendueles, C. (2018). Podemos, the Upheaval of Spanish Politics and the Challenge of Populism. *Journal of Contemporary European Studies 26*(1), 99–116. https://doi.org/10.1080/14782804.2017.1304899

Solorio, I., Ortega, J., Romero, R., and Guzmán, J. (2021). AMLO's Populism in Mexico and the Framing of the Extractivist Agenda: The Construction of the Hegemony of the People without the Indigenous Voices. *Zeitschrift für*

Vergleichende Politikwissenschaft 15(2), 249–273. https://doi.org/10.1007/s12286-021-00486-5

Stanley, B. (2008). The Thin Ideology of Populism. *Journal of Political Ideologies 13*(1), 95–110. https://doi.org/10.1080/13569310701822289

Staufer, S. J. (2021). Donald Trump, Bernie Sanders and the Question of Populism. *Journal of Political Ideologies 26*(2), 220–238. https://doi.org/10.1080/13569317.2020.1855777

Stockemer, D. (2019). *Populism Around the World: A Comparative Perspective.* Springer. https://doi.org/10.1007/978-3-319-96758-5

Surel, S. (2019). How to Stay Populist? The Front National and the Changing French Party System. *West European Politics 42*(6), 1230–1257. https://doi.org/10.1080/01402382.2019.1596693

Taggart, P. A. (2000). *Populism.* Open University Press.

Taggart, P. A. (2004). Populism and Representative Politics in Contemporary Europe. *Journal of Political Ideologies 9*(3), 269–288. https://doi.org/10.1080/1356931042000263528

Tosun, J., and Debus, M. (2021). Right-Wing Populist Parties and Environmental Politics: Insights from the Austrian Freedom Party's Support for the Glyphosate Ban. *Environmental Politics 30*(1–2), 224–244. https://doi.org/10.1080/09644016.2020.1813997

Tremlett, G. (2015, Mar 31). The Podemos Revolution: How a Small Group of Radical Academics Changed European Politics. *The Guardian.* www.theguardian.com/world/2015/mar/31/podemos-revolution-radical-academics-changed-european-politics

Trump, D. J. (2016, Apr 14). Let Me Ask America a Question. *Wall Street Journal.* www.wsj.com/articles/let-me-ask-america-a-question-1460675882

Trump, D. J. (2017a, Jun 1). Remarks Announcing United States Withdrawal From the United Nations Framework Convention on Climate Change Paris Agreement. *The American Presidency Project.* www.presidency.ucsb.edu/node/328739

Trump, D. J. (2017b, Aug 15). Executive Order 13807 – Establishing Discipline and Accountability in the Environmental Review and Permitting Process for Infrastructure Projects. *The American Presidency Project.* www.presidency.ucsb.edu/node/329622

Trump, D. J. (2017c, Aug 3). Remarks at a 'Make America Great Again' Rally in Huntington, West Virginia. *The American Presidency Project.* www.presidency.ucsb.edu/node/330949

Trump, D. J. (2017d, Jul 25). Remarks at a 'Make America Great Again' Rally in Youngstown, Ohio. *The American Presidency Project.* www.presidency.ucsb.edu/node/331396

Trump, D. J. (2017e, Sep 6). Remarks at Andeavor's Mandan Refinery in Mandan, North Dakota. *The American Presidency Project.* www.presidency.ucsb.edu/node/331141

Trump, D. J. (2017f, Oct 12). Proclamation 9659 – National Energy Awareness Month, 2017. *The American Presidency Project.* www.presidency.ucsb.edu/node/331273

Trump, D. J. (2017g, Jan 24). Executive Order 13766 – Expediting Environmental Reviews and Approvals for High-Priority Infrastructure

Projects. *The American Presidency Project.* www.presidency.ucsb.edu/node/322146

Trump, D. J. (2017h, Mar 27). Background Briefing on the President's Energy Independence Executive Order. *The American Presidency Project.* www.presidency.ucsb.edu/node/326556

Trump, D. J. (2017i, Mar 15). Remarks at a 'Make America Great Again' Rally in Nashville, Tennessee. *The American Presidency Project.* www.presidency.ucsb.edu/node/326412

Trump, D. J. (2017j, Mar 27). Remarks at the Conservative Political Action Conference in National Harbor, Maryland. www.govinfo.gov/content/pkg/DCPD-201700137/html/DCPD-201700137.html

Trump, D. J. (2017k, May 23). Press Briefing by OMB Director Mick Mulvaney on the FY2018 Budget. *The American Presidency Project.* www.presidency.ucsb.edu/node/328409

Trump, D. J. (2017l, Jun 12). Remarks During a Cabinet Meeting. *The American Presidency Project.* www.presidency.ucsb.edu/node/330935

Trump, D. J. (2018, Sep 28). Proclamation 9794 – National Energy Awareness Month, 2018. *The American Presidency Project.* www.presidency.ucsb.edu/node/333203

Trump, D. J. (2019a, Sep 30). Proclamation 9939 – National Energy Awareness Month, 2019. *The American Presidency Project.* www.presidency.ucsb.edu/node/333921

Trump, D. J. (2019b, Oct 23). Remarks at the Ninth Annual Shale Insight Conference in Pittsburgh, Pennsylvania. *The American Presidency Project.* www.presidency.ucsb.edu/node/333984

Trump, D. J. (2019c, Aug 13). Remarks on American Energy and Manufacturing at the Shell Pennsylvania Chemicals Plant in Monaca, Pennsylvania. *The American Presidency Project.* www.presidency.ucsb.edu/node/333787

Trump, D. J. (2019d, Jul 8). Remarks on the Environment. *The American Presidency Project.* www.presidency.ucsb.edu/node/333697

Trump, D. J. (2019e, Sep 12). Remarks at the House Republican Conference Member Retreat Dinner in Baltimore, Maryland. *The American Presidency Project.* www.presidency.ucsb.edu/node/333852

Trump, D. J. (2020a, Sep 30). Proclamation 10089 – National Energy Awareness Month, 2020. *The American Presidency Project.* www.presidency.ucsb.edu/node/343964

Trump, D. J. (2020b, Jul 16). Remarks by President Trump on Rolling Back Regulations to Help All Americans. *Trump White House Archives.* https://trumpwhitehouse.archives.gov/briefings-statements/remarks-president-trump-rolling-back-regulations-help-americans/

Trump, D. J. (2020c, May 29). Proclamation 10048 – National Ocean Month. *The American Presidency Project.* https://www.presidency.ucsb.edu/documents/proclamation-10048-national-ocean-month-2020

Turkewitz, J. (2017, Dec 4). Trump Slashes Size of Bears Ears and Grand Staircase Monuments. *The New York Times.* www.nytimes.com/2017/12/04/us/trump-bears-ears.html?module=inline

United Nations. (2020, Sep 24). Venezuela – President Addresses General Debate, 75th Session [Video]. *YouTube.* www.youtube.com/watch?v=0c3zjeEzp8w

Venezuela. (2013, Dec 4). Ley del Plan de la Patria: Segundo Plan Socialista de Desarrollo Económico y Social de la Nación 2013–2019 (No 6.118 Extraordinario). *The Grantham Research Institute on Climate Change and the Environment*. https://climate-laws.org/documents/law-of-the-plan-for-the-homeland-the-second-socialist-plan-of-social-and-economic-development-of-the-nation-2013-2019_4e83?id=law-of-the-plan-for-the-homeland-the-second-socialist-plan-of-social-and-economic-development-of-the-nation-2013-2019_3f0f

Vihma, A., Reischl, G., and Nonbo Andersen, A. (2021). A Climate Backlash: Comparing Populist Parties' Climate Policies in Denmark, Finland, and Sweden. *The Journal of Environment & Development 30*(3), 219–239. https://doi.org/10.1177/10704965211027748

Weyland, K. (2001). Clarifying a Contested Concept: Populism in the Study of Latin American Politics. *Comparative Politics 34*(1), 1–22. https://doi.org/10.2307/422412

Wike, R. (2017, Apr 21). 5 Charts Showing Where France's National Front Draws Its Support. *Pew Research Center*. www.pewresearch.org/short-reads/2017/04/21/5-charts-showing-where-frances-national-front-draws-its-support/

Wiseman, C., and Béland, D. (2010). The Politics of Institutional Change in Venezuela: Oil Policy During the Presidency Of Hugo Chávez. *Canadian Journal of Latin American and Caribbean Studies/Revue Canadienne des Études Latino-Américaines et Caraïbes 35*(70), 141–164. https://doi.org/10.1080/08263663.2010.12059263

Wong, W. (2018, Jun 20). 'The Menace Is Inequality:' A Conversation with Podemos's Pablo Iglesias. *The Nation*. www.thenation.com/article/archive/menace-inequality-conversation-podemoss-pablo-iglesias/

Yan, P., Schroeder, R., and Stier, S. (2021). Is There a Link Between Climate Change Scepticism and Populism? An Analysis of Web Tracking and Survey Data from Europe and the US. *Information, Communication & Society 25*(10), 1400–1439. https://doi.org/10.1080/1369118X.2020.1864005

Zúquete, J. P. (2008). The Missionary Politics of Hugo Chávez. *Latin American Politics and Society 50*(1), 91–121. https://doi.org/10.1111/j.1548-2456.2008.00005.x

Index

82   *Index*

For Product Safety Concerns and Information please contact our EU
representative GPSR@taylorandfrancis.com
Taylor & Francis Verlag GmbH, Kaufingerstraße 24, 80331 München, Germany